HOMER

THE
ODYSSEY

NOTES

COLES EDITORIAL BOARD

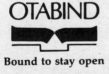

Bound to stay open

Publisher's Note

Otabind (Ota-bind). This book has been bound using the patented Otabind process. You can open this book at any page, gently run your finger down the spine, and the pages will lie flat.

ABOUT COLES NOTES

COLES NOTES have been an indispensible aid to students on five continents since 1948.

COLES NOTES are available for a wide range of individual literary works. Clear, concise explanations and insights are provided along with interesting interpretations and evaluations.

Proper use of COLES NOTES will allow the student to pay greater attention to lectures and spend less time taking notes. This will result in a broader understanding of the work being studied and will free the student for increased participation in discussions.

COLES NOTES are an invaluable aid for review and exam preparation as well as an invitation to explore different interpretive paths.

COLES NOTES are written by experts in their fields. It should be noted that any literary judgement expressed herein is just that — the judgement of one school of thought. Interpretations that diverge from, or totally disagree with any criticism may be equally valid.

COLES NOTES are designed to supplement the text and are not intended as a substitute for reading the text itself. Use of the NOTES will serve not only to clarify the work being studied, but should enhance the reader's enjoyment of the topic.

ISBN 0 - 7740 - 3332 - 0

© COPYRIGHT 1993 AND PUBLISHED BY
COLES PUBLISHING COMPANY
TORONTO—CANADA
PRINTED IN CANADA

Manufactured by Webcom Limited
Cover finish: Webcom's Exclusive **Duracoat**

CONTENTS

2000 1900 1800 1700 1600 1500 1400 1300 1200 1100 1000 900 800 700 600 500 400 300 200 100 0 100 200 300 400 500

FAR EAST

- 2000 ARYAN INVASION (INDIA)
- SHANG DYNASTY (CHINA)
- VEDIC PERIOD BEGINS (INDIA)
- THE BRAHMANAS (INDIA)
- BUDDHA (INDIA) CONFUCIUS (CHINA)
- INVADED BY ALEXANDER
- FA HSIEN (CHINA)

EGYPT

- HYKSOS INVASION
- HEIGHT OF EGYPTIAN POWER
- AKHNATON
- COLLAPSE OF POWER
- 525 ASSIMILATED INTO PERSIAN EMPIRE

HEBREWS

- ABRAHAM
- JOSEPH IN EGYPT
- MOSES
- SOLOMON'S DEATH DIVISION OF KINGDOM
- BABYLONIAN WARS

MESOPOTAMIA

- CODE OF HAMMURABI
- BABYLONIAN DYNASTY
- HITTITES TAKE NINEVAH
- HITTITE EMPIRE FALLS
- ASSYRIA CONQUERS MEDES
- MEDES DOMINANT
- THE AVESTA
- CYRUS

GREECE

- AGE OF PALACES
- CRETO-MINOAN ERA BEGINS LINEAR A WRITING
- MYCENAEN ERA BEGINS
- TROY FALLS DORIAN INVASION
- CITY STATES
- HOMER
- 495-406 SOPHOCLES
- 427-347 PLATO
- ALEXANDER'S CONQUESTS
- SELEUCID, PTOLEMAIC RULERS
- PLUTARCH
- JULIAN

2000 1900 1800 1700 1600 1500 1400 1300 1200 1100 1000 900 800 700 600 500 400 300 200 100 0 100 200 300 400 500

GREECE
WITH CONTEMPORARY CIVILIZATIONS

- ROMULUS
- ROME BUILT
- REPUBLIC BEGINS
- LIVIUS ANDRONICUS ROMAN LIT. BEGINS
- CICERO
- 27 EMPIRE BEGINS
- VIRGIL
- GOTHIC INVASION
- EMPIRE DIVIDED
- EMPIRE ENDS

ROME

THE MEDITERRANEAN AND HOMER'S GREECE

A route of Odysseus' travels

When Odysseus passes the Peloponnesus (southern Greece) he enters the world of Homer's poetic fantasy—some writers (M. Victor Bérard, for one) have, however, used geographical clues in Homer's descriptions to reconstruct the route. This is entirely conjecture but serves as an interesting frame of reference.

1. TROY (or Ilium): city of the great ten year's war of which Homer's Iliad is a partial description.

BOOK IX
2. ISMAROS: land of the Kikones.
3. THE LOTOS EATERS.
4. CYCLOPS: the cave of Polyphemos.

BOOK X
5. AIOLOS: floating island home of the God of the Winds.
6. LAISTRYGONIA: Land of Cannibals ruled by King Lamos.
7. CIRCE: the Isle of Aiaia, home of the witch.

BOOK XI
8. LAND OF THE KIMMERIANS: entrance to the Underworld.

BOOK XII
9. ISLANDS OF THE SIRENS.
10. SKYLLA AND KHARYBDIS.
11. LAND OF HELIOS HYPERION.
12. PILLARS OF HERAKLES: leaving the land of Helios, Odysseus' ship is wrecked by a storm and his men

lost. Patching the ship himself he is driven back through Skylla and Kharybdis where the ship is lost. Odysseus says that he drifts for nine days and nights before he is washed up on the shore of Kalypso's island; it is sometimes thought that the currents took him to the Pillars of Herakles, "the end of the earth."

BOOK V
13. KALYPSO: the island of Ogygia. It is here that the reader first meets Odysseus.

BOOKS VI–XII
14. PHAEACIA: the island of King Alkinoos; it is here, after the games of Book VIII that Odysseus relates the adventures which comprise Books IX–XII.

BOOKS I–IV & XIII–XXIV
15. ITHAKA: the island-kingdom of Odysseus. It is here that the poem begins with the travels of Telemakhos; Odysseus-himself arrives home in Book XIII.

PLOT DIAGRAM

	BOOK	LOCATION	EVENT	TIME
Telemachiad	I	Ithaka	PALLAS ATHENA PERSUADES TELEMAKHOS TO SEEK HIS FATHER	one day
	II			one day
	III	Pylos	TELEMAKHOS VISITS NESTOR	one day
	IV	Sparta	TELEMAKHOS VISITS MENELAOS AND HELEN	one day
Wanderings of Odysseus	V	Ogygia	HERMES ORDERS KALYPSO TO FREE ODYSSEUS	twenty-one days
	VI	Phaiakia	ODYSSEUS' RAFT-WRECK; ARRIVAL IN PHAIAKIA	
	VII		WELCOMED BY NAUSIKAA AND ALKINOOS	one day
	VIII		GAMES	one day
	IX		ODYSSEUS RELATES HIS ADVENTURES	one day / related time: ten years
	X			
	XI			
	XII			
Return of Odysseus	XIII	Ithaka	ARRIVAL IN ITHAKA--EUMAOS' HUT	seven days
	XIV		RETURN OF TELEMAKHOS	
	XV			
	XVI		MEETING OF ODYSSEUS AND TELEMAKHOS	
	XVII		ODYSSEUS DISGUISED AS BEGGAR	
	XVIII		FIGHT WITH IROS	
	XIX		EURYKLEIA LEARNS ODYSSEUS' IDENTITY	
	XX		THE BANQUET	
	XXI		THE CONTEST OF THE BOW	
	XXII		SLAYING OF THE SUITORS	
	XXIII		ODYSSEUS REVEALS HIMSELF TO PENELOPE	
	XXIV		PEACE	

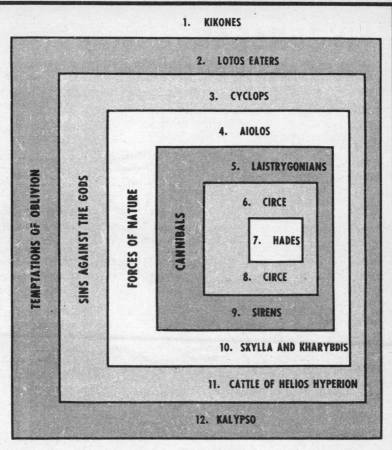

1. KIKONES
2. LOTOS EATERS
3. CYCLOPS
4. AIOLOS
5. LAISTRYGONIANS
6. CIRCE
7. HADES
8. CIRCE
9. SIRENS
10. SXYLLA AND KHARYBDIS
11. CATTLE OF HELIOS HYPERION
12. KALYPSO
13. PHAIAKIA

EARTHLY AND SUPERNATURAL CITIES: WAR AND PEACE

TEMPTATIONS OF OBLIVION

SINS AGAINST THE GODS

FORCES OF NATURE

CANNIBALS

SYMMETRY IN THE ODYSSEY

Odysseus' 13 adventures (including 2 visits to Circe) conform to the geometric ideal of ancient Greek design. Hades becomes the center of the epic structure and moving outward, the action develops in perfect concentricity (see pp. 71-72).

MYCENAEAN SAILING VESSEL

ODYSSEUS' SHIP AS IT MAY HAVE APPEARED
composite representation based upon illustrations found on Mycenaean art objects

A. **BEAK**- marks prow, comparable to bowspirit on 19th-century whaling vessels

B. **EYES**- believed to ward off evil, comparable to Gorgoneion on armor

C. **OARS**- used for maneuvering and as supplement to sail

D. **RUDDER**- shaped like an extra-long oar

E. **DECKS**- only at prow and stern; the galley would be in a small area set off, probably in the prow

F. **CREW**- freemen rather than slaves; the number of rowers would depend on the size of the ship

G. **HOLD**- cargo and supplies would be carried in the body of the ship; no cabins

CLASSICAL AND MYCENAEAN ARMOR

ABOVE: Traditional concept of Homeric heroes established centuries later in paintings and statuary of "Classical" Greece.

RIGHT: Armor used in the Trojan War; illustration based upon a suit of Mycenaean armor discovered recently at Dendra:

A. HELMET........bronze or leather, with matched carved boar's tusks sewn on, and horse-tail for decoration. NOTE: no visor or neck guard.

B. SWORD............worn over shoulder, size and design determined by owner.

C. SHIELD...." figure-eight "design, leather stretched over framework of sticks.

D. CORSLET.......bronze, with traditional Gorgon's head believed to avert evil.

E. APRON.......soft leather, design and style reflecting the taste of the owner.

F. GREAVES...........leather or bronze, attached by thongs, to guard the shins.

SOURCE: Archeological Reports 1960-61 pages 9-11; Frank H. Stubbings'

"Arms and Armor"in Wace and Stubbings' A Companion to Homer pages 504-522.

ILLUSTRATED BY THE AUTHOR, GUY DAVENPORT, Ph. D.

GREECE
and the Agean

THRACE

MACEDONIA

TROY •   TROAD

Lemnos

• MT. OLYMPOS

Lesbos

THESSALY

Skyros

H E L L A S

EUBOEA

Chios

AULIS
BOEOTIA

DELPHI •

• THEBES

ATTICA

CORINTH •

• ATHENS

Cyclades

MYCENAE •

Delos

• ARGOS

ARCADIA

Melos

• SPARTA

PYLOS •

Scale: 100 miles

• Ios

KNOSSOS
Crete   TYLISSOS

HOMER: A BIOGRAPHY OF LEGENDS

It is unfortunate that we are sure of nothing about Homer. The ancient Greeks themselves seem to have known very little, but, as was often the case with honored men, many stories were circulated about him. These may be wholly fiction, but they may also contain some truth; we will probably never find out.

Several ancient cities claimed to be the birthplace of Homer, and there was similar disagreement about the time when he lived. It is generally agreed by scholars today that he was born somewhere in Ionia (the Greek west coast of Asia Minor), probably during the eighth century B.C. There may be some truth in the story of his blindness, for if the ancient tradition that Homer was the author of the Hymn to Delian Apollo is true, then he was blind. Near the end of the Hymn, the poet speaks to the girls who serve the Temple of Apollo on Delos:

> "Think of me in the future, whenever any person
> who has much experience comes here and asks you,
> 'Girls, which man sings most sweetly of the bards
> who come here, and whom do you like most to hear?'
> You must answer all together: 'A blind man, who lives
> in stony Chios, and whose songs will always be the
> finest.' "

There are references to his death in later Greek writers, but they may be based on traditions handed down from an earlier period. Although the many stories about Homer are probably no more than legends, and can furnish no real evidence for his life, we do know something about the period in which he probably lived (see "Homer's Ionia," below).

COMPLETE BACKGROUND

Introduction

An epic, Aristotle says, is a poem about men in action. Ezra Pound, a modern poet and student of the classical tradition, defines the form as "a poem containing history." As will be seen, the archaeological discovery of the ruins of Troy has confirmed the basic accuracy of Homer's account, but "action" is the real concern of both the poet and today's reader. The *Odyssey* and the *Iliad* record a geography of the Mediterranean, but more important they reflect the character of every people known to the Greeks, and veritably every human activity and emotion. In the *Iliad,* although the city of Troy as setting would seem to limit Homer's scope, it is here that the world's greatest heroes and gods convene; in the *Odyssey,* man confronts Nature: the world and its gods. Few works of literature have managed to achieve so broad a panorama of scene, national character, and human emotion; in this, the *Iliad* and the *Odyssey* are rivaled only by Cervantes' *Don Quixote,* the plays of Shakespeare, and Tolstoy's *War and Peace.* Humanity will always live with the questions, "What is a good man? A good woman? A good society?" Homer's answers are of permanent value.

Indeed, the greatness of the poetry lies in its wise attitude toward the life of man: of man at odds with men, of man at odds with his world. This, in turn, is enhanced by the matchless skill with which the story is told: never hurriedly, and yet never with a wasted word. Its diction is simple and exact; its lines, compact with action and detail. While three lines removed at random from a modern novel or poem might often be obscure, even incomprehensible, three lines removed at random from Homer are invariably comprehensible, frequently even memorable.

The Historical Background

Mycenaean Greece   Achilles and Odysseus, Menelaos and Agamemnon, Helen and Paris, historical or not, are figures of the late Bronze Age in Greece in the twelfth century B.C. For Homer, in the eighth century, they represented a distant past which had become so glorified in song and legend as to be "heroic." History confirms that these Mycenaeans were indeed a mighty people: in the last generations before the "Dorian Invasion" (see below) they had extended a military and economic domain to include the islands of the Aegean, the Crete of the older Minoan empire, and even seem to have attacked Egypt. The Mycenaeans even knew and used the art of writing (see "The Linear B Tablets," below); they built mighty palaces of stone and had a political geography, the complexity of which is indicated in the *Iliad's* famous "Catalogue of Ships" and which is substantiated (though with altered particulars) in the written records found in the Mycenaean capitals of Pylos and Mycenae and in the Mycenaean-occupied Knossos on Crete.

Geography in Homer   In the eighteenth and early nineteenth centuries, it was thought that the world Homer describes was hardly more real than Alice's Wonderland. Though Athens is mentioned in both the epics, and Sparta (also called by its alternate name Lacedaimon) and several other locations still exist, it was assumed that Mycenae, Troy, and the fabulous cities of Crete (such as Knossos and Phaistos) were entirely mythical. In 1870, however, Heinrich Schliemann (1822-1890) began to dig in Turkey at a site which Homer's text seemed to indicate, and uncovered a burned city of some antiquity which he called Troy. Although he had not dug down far enough, and had actually discovered a much later city built over Troy's ruins, he is given credit for the discovery.

Six years later, Schliemann went to the Greek mainland and uncovered Agamemnon's city Mycenae, to the astonishment of the world. Here he found many golden weapons and containers, together with what has been traditionally called the golden death-mask of Agamemnon. In 1881, he uncovered Orchomenos and in 1885, Tiryns, cities in the Argive plain, both mentioned in the *Iliad*.

Between 1900 and 1908, Sir Arthur Evans (1851-1941), a British archaeologist, uncovered the beautiful Cretan palace of Minos at Knossos. Carl W. Blegen, the American archaeologist, has discovered and excavated sandy Pylos, Nestor's palace and city. These and other discoveries of this century have changed the entire conception of the reality of Homer's world, for suddenly it was not only very real but utterly strange and beautiful —and nothing at all like the Greece of Athens in the classical fifth century.

Before the archaeological finds were firmly within the

minds of the scholars, an engaging French senator and Homeric scholar named Victor Bérard (1864-1931) came up with the theory that Homer had not himself traveled a great deal, but that he had before him a map of the world such as the Phoenician merchants must have used, sailing all over the known world at that time. His map would not have looked like a modern one; it would be all coastline for the most part, and would show a rough notion of the coasts of the Mediterranean, with the seaports, islands, and shipping routes marked. We know of one such map, that of Hanno, though it is of a much later date. Using the map as a guide to his imagination (see rendering on p. 5 of the route conjectured in Bérard's *L'Odyssée d'Homère*, Paris, 1931), he turned Stromboli into Polyphemos the giant thrower of rocks, the opium-smoking Algerians into the Lotos Eaters, the island Aiaia ("Land of Grief") into the haunt of the witch Circe ("She-hawk" in Greek), and so on. This theory, of course, cannot be proved but is thought-provoking and gives us a hint as to how Homer might have taken real things that he had never seen and transformed them into the stuff that good stories are made of.

Linear B Script   The archaeologists and speculators like Bérard, however, gave us only the physical presence of Homer's world. It had no voice until Michael Ventris, a young English architect and amateur linguist, cracked the writing that had been found by Sir Arthur Evans at Knossos and Carl Blegen at Pylos—the famous Linear B script (so named to distinguish it from the earlier Linear A; the script itself is that used by the "Minoans," whose language continues to defy decipherment).

        Ventris' discovery in 1952 shook the scholarly world, for it established (a) that Cretans in late Minoan times were familiar with a Greek vocabulary, for much of the Linear B is recognizable Greek written in a different and earlier alphabet (the Greek alphabet itself evolved much later out of contact with the Phoenicians), and (b) that Crete, far from being a separate empire from mainland Greece, was, just as Homer says, part of a large empire of Minoan and Mycenaean people, with the capitals of a system of kingdoms at Mycenae, Pylos, and Knossos. It used to be thought preposterous that Homer, "whoever he was," could write. We now know, however, that the written word was an important part of this distant past (the tablets at Pylos seem to have been written some four or five hundred years *before* Homer). The approximately 3500 tablets which have been recovered are inventories of cattle, ships, armour (all like Homer's own catalogues); the interested student should investigate the writings of John Chadwick, Leonard R. Palmer, and Joseph Alsop in the BIBLIOGRAPHY.

The People in Homer   The late Mycenaean world which Homer's poetry celebrates had existed centuries before him, and his knowledge of those times would have come from the oral tradition and other epics. Through modern archaeology, however, we may know more about the twelfth-century world of Homer's characters than he did himself in the eighth century.

"Kings," for example, in that "heroic" era, were no more than tribal chieftains. They maintained loose leagues among themselves for commercial intercourse and periodic common defense, but politics seem to have been otherwise quite primitive. Sculpture was somewhat crude and, for the most part, religious; vases and urns were decorated but these, too, were more functional than artistic. Weapons were bronze and wooden spears, bows and arrows (see illustration, p. 9). For a careful discussion of these early arts, see Friedrich Matz's *The Art of Crete and Early Greece*.

Neither were there great cities at this time; the mainland kings lived in fortified stone citadels and the townspeople in villages outside the walls, came into the royal stronghold only in time of war. The remains of some of these citadels— Mycenae, Tiryns, and Pylos—furnish much information; many details are as Homer describes them.

There has been much speculation over the centuries about the appearance of Homer's heroes. The conventions of painting, of book illustrations, and of heroic statuary have provided the physical details of the traditional character, but archaeology has changed a great deal of this conception. For example, the famous horse-mane helmet, with its curved crest mounted above a helmet with visor and cheek-pieces, is much later than Odysseus' time. Odysseus, we now know, would have worn a peaked leather cap with small bronze or boar's tusk ivory plates sewn to it like fish scales and resembling medieval chain mail. The attached horse tail hung from the top and trailed down the warrior's back (see p. 9). His other armor would have been similarly mounted on leather. His clothes would have been brightly colored and embroidered with geometric designs; brief shirts were the undergarment; in cold weather woolen cloaks were worn and sandals were exchanged for warm boots.

Homer testifies that the Achaeans (his name for all Greeks) were a clean people, and honored the beauty of the body. They had no soap, but bathed in tubs of warm water and annointed themselves with a perfumed oil, the manufacture of which was the chief industry of the Mycenaean-Minoan Empire. We are not sure of what racial strain these people were. Many of them (Odysseus, Menelaos, and Helen, for instance) had hair that was yellow or red, certainly blond.

The best source nevertheless, for knowing *how* Homer's people lived is still Homer's poems, for it must be remembered that they are *poetic* people: the *Odyssey is* literature. And yet we are offered great and reliable detail as to the practice of religion and sacrifices to and attitudes toward the gods, interiors of the dwellings, ships, clothing and foods—the physical realities of everyday life almost 3,000 years ago.

The Gods in Homer   The Greeks differed from the gods themselves in that the gods were immortal and were endowed with magical powers—there was little else to distinguish them from the lusty, jealous, hateful, hungry, and thirsty human beings below the not-so-lofty Mount Olympos. Literally, too, were the gods akin to men: many of the Greek gods were notorious in their seduction of the mortals, and in many an epic a mythical human being takes great pride in his superhuman lineage. The behavior of the gods, however, did not fully determine the character of religious observance which was, officially, most reverent.

There were twelve Olympian gods (whose home was a city atop Mount Olympos), the king of whom was *Zeus* (whose name means simply "The Bright One"). Of these gods, Homer makes reference to *Pallas Athena*, goddess of the intelligence; *Aphrodite*, goddess of love; *Apollo*, god of light, music, and healing; *Ares*, god of war; *Poseidon*, god of the sea; *Artemis*, god of animals; *Hera*, goddess of mothers; *Hermes*, god of voyages; *Hebe*, goddess of children; and *Hephaistos*, god of fire.

Among the gods of the underworld were *Demeter*, goddess of ripened grain; her daughter *Persephone*, goddess of plant fertility; and *Dionysos*, god of wine. Because this Chthonic ("underground") religion was one of great mystery and secretiveness, we know far less about it than we do of the official public Zeus-religion.

Then there were countless minor dieties, such as *Leukothea*, a sea nymph who helps Odysseus, and *Thetis*, the sea-nymph mother of Achilles who entreats Zeus on his behalf. In fact, everything growing or moving was or contained an immortal spirit: springs, rivers, trees, the sun, moon, sea, and the mountains all were gods. The world was the Greek "church," and every phenomenon was interpreted as divinity in action.

The Dorian Invasions Through the height of power and the twilight of the Mycenaean Age a people from the north of Greece, the Dorians, had been slowly and peacefully moving down into the Greek mainland. At this same time, the Mycenaean civilization was weakening from internal strife (as represented by the war against Thebes in the *Theban Cycle*—see "Other Greek Epics," below) and by wars waged for wealth against the Trojans and others. The ten-year Trojan War was hardly a victory for the Mycenaeans, who seem to have exhausted themselves; the end of the war was followed by an increase in pressure from the Dorians and about 1100 B.C. came an almost total conquest of the Greek mainland and the Peloponnesseus. The great cities of Mycenae, Pylos, and Tiryns, for example, were totally destroyed; only Athens was able to withstand the Dorians and remain a center of Mycenaean culture.

The Dark Ages and   From about 1100 to 800 B.C. is the period
the Ionian Migration   of the so-called "Dark Age" of Greek
                           history, "dark" because we know very
little of the times: rough, crude pottery is the only real record
we have of this "sub-Mycenaean" culture. The art of writing
was forgotten and the great stone palaces were replaced with
mud brick structures.

All traces of the Mycenaeans, however, were not wiped
out in the invasion and occupation. The "Ionian Migration," a
slow movement of people from the Greek mainland to the west
coast of Asia Minor, took with it, preserved, and continued to
develop the older culture.

Homer's Ionia   The eighth-century world in which Homer
                       lived, though little more than four centuries
distant from that of his Mycenaean heroes, contrasted greatly
with that "heroic" age. The Ionian civilization was one of a
highly-developed sophistication in spite of its being predom-
inantly agricultural. Having lost the older, Linear B writing,
they adapted the Phoenician alphabet and inaugurated a cultural revival.

The Ionians founded cities which were completely independent of each other and of the mainland. Most of the citizens
were farmers and herdsmen (in the *Odyssey* there is the careful
distinction between shepherds, swineherds, and goatherds—so
specialized was their agrarian society). There were merchants
and sailors, since trade with other areas in the Mediterranean
area was reviving, and there were many craftsmen: carpenters,
potters, and armorers; there is no evidence for large shops, however, and most essentials were made in the homes.

One of the classes of specialists was that of the wandering bards (*aoidoi*), such as Homer, who made their living by
travelling through the various Greek settlements, reciting their
versions of the epics or "songs" which celebrated the Mycenaean
past as do the *Iliad* and *Odyssey*.

As well as giving us an idea of life in Mycenaean times,

these epics also furnish us with evidence about life in Homer's own time. It is especially in the similes and descriptive passages that the life and preoccupations of Ionian Greeks in the eighth century are revealed.

The Making of the Epic

The Composition   Some of the songs recited by the *aoidoi* seem to have been preserved since Mycenaean times; others undoubtedly originated during the Dark Age. Homer thus worked in a literary tradition very like that of the modern ballad singer and was free to quote lines and even long passages that existed in other ballads or poems. Homer's materials, as writing had been lost, had been preserved orally; the tales were memorized and sung from memory so that, through the generations, many changes in the materials were undoubtably lost, changed, or fabricated. Quotations from Homer in the texts of Aristophanes, Plato, and Aristotle show that their "Homer" was widely variant from that which has come down to us. For a discussion of the method of oral composition, see "The Epic Formula," below.

Other Greek Epics   Scholars now generally believe that the following epics were all written after Homer's *Iliad* and *Odyssey*. Both Homer and the others, however, took their plots and characters from pre-existing materials of the oral tradition. The later poets have attempted to supply enough information to Homer to complete the *Trojan* or *Homeric Cycle*: a telling of the stories of the war and its aftermath in a chronological and complete account. Several epic cycles seem to have existed, dealing with the adventures of *Theseus* (who slew the Minotaur in the Labyrinth of King Minos' palace), of *Perseus* (who slew the snake-haired gorgon Medusa), and of *Minos* (who owned the monstrous human flesh-eating bull from the sea). There were lengthy legends dealing with *Bellerophon* (who rode the winged horse Pegasus and slew the Chimaera) and with the great labors of *Herakles;* the *Argonautica* which dealt with the adventures of *Jason* and his men of Argos who sailed into a land of fantasy (very like that of the *Odyssey*) in search of the fabulous golden fleece. We know, too, of the

Theban Cycle, three epics dealing with *King Oedipos* of Thebes, the curse his crime of parricide and marriage of his mother brought upon that city and the later battle for the city by Oedipos' sons in the "Seven Against Thebes" epic. Many of these epics have been lost and their authors are either unknown or disputed; references to the epics by other or later authors are often the only inkling of their existence (the "Theban Cycle" is no longer extant but is reported to have been preserved by Sophocles in his Oedipos Trilogy, the fifth-century plays *Oedipos Rex, Antigone,* and *Oedipos at Colonos.*

As it can be reconstructed, the *Homeric Cycle* seems to have consisted of some eight epics: (1) the KYPRIA celebrated the flight of Paris and Helen from Sparta before the outbreak of the war; it contains the story of the judgment of Paris after the wedding of Thetis at which Athena, Hera, and Aphrodite quarreled over who was to claim the golden apple inscribed "for the fairest." (b) the ILIAD of Homer describes approximately fifty days of the war. (c) the AITHIOPIS was a continuation of the war, from the funeral of Hektor to the death of Achilles. (d) the ILIAS PARVA ("the little Iliad") offers the account of Odysseus' Trojan Horse ruse to enter the city, the contest for Achilles' armor between Aias and Odysseus. (e) the ILIUM PERSIS portrayed the sack of Troy, the entrance into the battle of Achilles' son, the deaths of Hecuba, Priam, the rape and abduction of Kassandra, etc. (f) the NOSTOI describes the homeward voyages of the various Greek leaders (with the exception of Odysseus) and the fates they meet at their homes—here the murder of Agamemnon by his unfaithful wife is described to be recounted in Aeschylos' fifth-century drama. (g) the ODYSSEY of Homer, the *nostos,* "homeward voyage," of Odysseus. (h) the TELEGONIA, named after its main figure, Telegonos, a son of Odysseus by Circe, who slays his father and eventually marries Penelope; this epic closes the *Homeric Cycle* with the marriage of Telemakhos (Odysseus' son by Penelope) and Circe— all four go to live on Circe's enchanted isle.

The Epic Formula   The oral phase through which the epics came in the Dark Age established a certain poetic technique required by the recitations of the bards or singers. The plots of the stories were traditional by Homer's

time and known to all, but the epics were not repeated ver-
batim—the plot or framework was established and unalterable,
but the details seem to have varied with each re-telling.

Approximately one-third of the lines in Homer's poetry
are repeated one or more times. The repetition is made possible
by the uniform metrical pattern of hexameter lines (eight ac-
cented feet to the line) which never conclude with a broken
thought; grammatical clauses are rarely continued from one
line to another so that the language operates in neat formulas.
Lines and verses may appear in whole, then, many times, their
insertion never disrupting the flow of the tight metrical rhythm.
Within the single lines are similarly formulized phrases of a
fixed metrical count, facilitating the repetition of the phrase.
Thus, for each poetic situation, there are epithet-name com-
pounds ready to fit the meter of the line: Dark-clouded Zeus,
Aegis-bearing Zeus, Father of gods and men, Son of Kronos,
Lord of lightning, etc. Achilles has some thirty-six different
epithets. In the oral tradition, such formulae lend themselves
easily to memorization and the singer has a ready-made phrase
for each metrical situation so that he can compose his song as
he goes. These formulas indicate to scholars the certainty that
the epics went through an oral stage; they testify to the plastic
state of the epics before they come to be written down. The
Greek epics were, indeed, a living poetry.

History of the Text   It is not certain how the present text differs
from that known to Greek antiquity. The
earliest known manuscript of Homer is that of the Marcian
Library at Venice, placed there in the fifteenth century by
Cardinal Bessarion, but the version we now have derives from
copies of the poems made by scholars in Alexandria in the first
two centuries of our era. Divergent texts seem to have been
harmonized by the Alexandrines, and it is possible that they
themselves divided the poem into twenty-four books (one for
each letter of the Greek alphabet); some scholars feel, however, that this division may have been Homer's own, as each
book is about the right length to have been sung in a single
evening. The student interested in the history of the *Iliad*, from
its first known presence to its first printing in 1488 by Demetrias
Damilas of Florence, will want to consult J. A. Davison's "The

Transmission of the Text," in Wace and Stubbings' *A Companion to Homer* (Oxford, 1963).

Names in Homer

The spellings in this volume follow, in great part, those of the Greek: for example, *Hektor* and *Menelaos* instead of the Latin *Hector* and *Menelaus*. In the eighteenth and nineteenth centuries, Latin was studied more than Greek, and most Greek literature was approached with a Latin point of view. Hence the traditional predilection for the Latin names of the gods; *Minerva* rather than *Pallas Athena, Mercury* rather than *Hermes,* etc. It is rapidly becoming the style among translators to render the names of Homer's characters as faithfully as possible to their appearance in the original Greek, but we shall probably always say *Homer* and not the *Homeros* to which he would have responded. In addition, it is difficult to be both consistent and clear in rendering the Greek into English; thus words such as *Aeschylus* and *Mycenae, Achilles* (for *Akhilleus*), which are familiar to us in the Latinized form, have been retained. The following chart clarifies transliterations and their different equivalents (difficult pronounciations are indicated.

GREEK	TRADITIONAL ENGLISH	LATIN
Akhaia	Achaea	Achaea
Akhaians	Achaeans	Achaeans
Akhilleus	Achilles	Achilles
Aiaia (eye-eye-a)	Aeaea	Aeaea
Aigisthos (uh-gisth-os)	Aegisthus	Aegisthus
Aiolos (eye-o-los)	Aeolus	Aeolus
Aias (eye-as)	Ajax	Ajax
Alkinoos (al-kin-o-os)	Alcinous	Alcinous
Antikleia (anti-kla-a)	Anticlea	Anticlea
Antinoös (an-tino-ös)	Antinous	Antinous
Aphrodite (aphrodite)	Aphrodite	Venus
Ares	Ares	Mars
Artemis	Artemis	Diana
Athena	Athene	Minerva
Autolykos (auotlikos)	Autolycus	Autolycus
Danaäns (danaäns)	Danaans	Danaans
Demeter (demeter)	Demeter	Ceres

GREEK	TRADITIONAL ENGLISH	LATIN
Demodokos	Demodocus	Demodocus
Dionysos (dionisos)	Dionysus	Bacchus
Eos (a-os)	Dawn	Aurora
Eumaios (you-mi-os)	Eumaeus	Eumaeus
Euryklei (your-ikla-a)	Eurycleia	Eurycleia
Eurymachus	Eurymachus	Eurymachus
Helen	Helen	Helena
Hellas	Greece	Graecia
Hephaistos (hephistos)	Hephaestus	Vulcan
Hera (Here-a)	Hera	Juno
Herakles (herakles)	Hercules	Hercules
Hermes (hermes)	Hermes	Mercury
Ilion	Troy	Ilium
Ithaka	Ithaca	Ithaca
Kalypso (kalipso)	Calypso	Calypso
Kharybdis (karibdis)	Charybdis	Charybdis
Khios	Chios	Chios
Kikones	Cicones	Cicones
Kimmeria	Cimmeria	Cimmeria
Kirke	Circe	Circe
Klytaimnestra (Klitemnestra)	Clytemnestra	Clytemnestra
Kronos	Cronus	Cronus
Lacedaimon	Sparta	Sparta
Laistrygonia (Lestrigonia)	Lestrygonia	Lestrygonia
Leukothea (Lewkotha-a)	Leucothea	Leucothea
Lotos	Lotus	Lotus
Melantheus (melanthe-us)	Melanthius	Melanthius
Menlaos (mene-la-os)	Menelaus	Menelaus
Nausikaä (now-si-kä)	Nausicaa	Nausicaa
Odysseus (o-dis-use)	Ulysses	Ulysses
Outis	No Man	
Pallas Athena (Athena)	Pallas Athene	Minerva
Parnassos	Parnassus	Parnassus
Patroklos	Patroclus	Patroclus
Persephone (persephone)	Persephone	Proserpina
Phaidra (fedra)	Phaedra	Phaedra
Philoitios (filoy-te-us)	Philoetius	Philoetius
Polyphemos (poli-phe-mos)	Polyphemus	Polyphemus
Poseidon (posidon)	Poseidon	Neptune
Skylla (skilla)	Scylla	Scylla
Sirenes	Sirens	Sirens
Telemakhos	Telemachus	Telemachus
Zeus (Zew-s)	Zeus	Jupiter

It is important, also, to understand that the Greeks of Homer's poetry had one name only, to which might be added (or substituted) the patronymic form (one's father's name with a special ending). Thus, *Odysseus Laertides* simply means *Odysseus, son of Laertes; Achilles Peliades* translates as *Achilles, son of Peleus*. And Greek names were frequently like those in Dickens: they tell something of the man's character. Odysseus means "The Wrathful"; he was so named by his grandfather Autolykos ("Wolf"). Hektor literally means "Mainstay." Interesting meanings, as they turn up, are noted in the "Commentary" through the COMPREHENSIVE SUMMARY, below.

CAPSULE SUMMARY

Odysseus, king of Ithaka, husband of Penelope and father of Telemakhos, had gone off to the Trojan War twenty years ago when the *Odyssey* begins. The war had lasted ten years; a series of extraordinary adventures have since kept Odysseus from returning to Ithaka. Book I opens prior to the hero's return, when he is with the nymph Kalypso far out at sea. Poseidon, the sea god, has kept Odysseus from returning because of a grudge (Odysseus, in self defense, blinded his giant son, Polyphemos, the Cyclops).

At a council of the gods, Pallas Athena, goddess of intelligence, asks permission to try to get the wily hero back to his faithful wife and son, who are in a quandary as to whether Penelope should assume that Odysseus is dead and marry again. The suitors pester her day and night and are eating the family into poverty. The gods agree, and Kalypso is ordered by Hermes to help Odysseus get home. Odysseus builds a ship and sets out. Poseidon sees him and tries to drown him. A nymph helps him swim to the land of the Phaeacians, a kindly people who listen to his recitation of his adventures (as do we), and bring him home to Ithaka.

Here he makes contact with his faithful swineherd, his son, and a few men needed to help him slay his wife's suitors. Penelope has finally despaired of her husband's return and has promised to marry the winner of an archery contest that requires the use of Odysseus' bow. But none of the suitors can even string the great bow. Odysseus, disguised as a beggar, strings the bow, slays the suitors, and discloses his identity. A blood feud between Odysseus and the relatives of the suitors is stopped by Pallas Athena, in the name of Zeus, and the poem ends with a scene of pastoral happiness. The lost is found, the wrongs are righted, the long suffering is over.

COMPREHENSIVE SUMMARY

Book I: Ithaka

COMMENTARY: The *Odyssey*—"Song of Odysseus" is what the title means to Greek ears—begins, as the Roman poet Horace (65-8 B.C.) says in his *Art of Poetry, in medias res,* "in the middle of things." Homer begins his story at a point in time when Odysseus' wanderings are all but over. We see at first hand his voyage from the island Ogygia and his return to his native Ithaka, but the rest of the adventures we see in what has come to be known as "flashback," narrated by Odysseus himself just before he returns home, while he is awaiting passage to Ithaka at the court of the Phaeacians. Not until the fifth book of the epic do we see Odysseus. The first four books are devoted to his son Telemakhos, now twenty years old, and his wife Penelope.

The epic opens with an invocation to the Muse Kalliope (not called upon here by name, although her name is found in later works), the goddess of epic poetry. She is the daughter of Zeus, the "father of gods and of men," as Homer calls him, and of Mnemosyne, the goddess of Memory.

COMMENTARY: If we think of the Greek gods as states of mind, we can see that they are scarcely the products of primitive superstition or the obsolete and discarded figures of a religion no longer believed in. As a matter of fact, we still believe very much in the Greek gods. When we say of a person that jealousy has made a raging monster of him, or of another that he is in love, or of another that he is gifted with a keen intelligence, we are saying that each has encountered a quality which we know to be permanent in human nature (jealousy, love, intelligence). The Greeks thought of these permanent qualities as gods and goddesses. They had minds less abstract and more tactile than ours. We have no visual or concrete way of dramatizing the inception of a brilliant idea (except the cartoonist's device of symbolizing it with a light bulb, or the gesture of slapping our foreheads in amazement). For the Greeks, a brilliant idea was the goddess Pallas Athena.

Because Odysseus' great quality as a man was his intelligence the most important god in the *Odyssey* is Pallas Athena (for whom the city of Athens was named and for whom the most beautiful of Greek temples, The Parthenon, was built). It is she who keeps alive in Odysseus the mental skill that is named in the first line of the *Odyssey—polytropos*. The word means "many turnings," in the sense of Odysseus having fertile plans, many ideas. W. H. D. Rouse translated it as "never at a loss." It is the quality of mind later imagined for Sherlock Holmes and Tarzan, and is still the western world's ideal for a hero's mind; Robinson Crusoe and James Bond are *polytropos*.

Homer asks the Muse to tell of the wanderings of Odysseus from the end of the Trojan War (where he was one of the most heroic of the Greek warriors) to the time when, ten years later, he came back home to Ithaka. (The war took ten years to win, so Odysseus has been away for twenty years.) We learn from the Invocation (the first ten lines of the epic) that Odysseus has suffered many hardships (thus ascribing to Odysseus the concomitant heroic quality of *tlemosune*, patient and tough endurance of pain and set-backs), that he has seen the "minds and towns of many men" (this would have fascinated the Greek listener, who depended on literature to tell him of the world beyond the confines of his village or town), and that Odysseus' men committed a great crime and were lost. Odysseus alone returned.

Then we are told briefly where Odysseus is at the moment. He has been kept for seven years by a goddess on the remotest of islands. Since her name is Kalypso ("the hider") and her island is named Ogygia ("the ancient place"), we are to understand that Odysseus is under a strong enchantment and that only divine help can free him.

The narrative part of the poem begins at a meeting of the Olympian gods on their mountain city. With a masterful stroke of drama Homer has the first speech of the poem spoken by Zeus himself. He is saying that men blame the gods for their misfortunes, whereas the truth is that men are fools who bring their own suffering on themselves. He tells the story of Aigisthos, who has murdered the King of the Greeks, Agamemnon.

COMMENTARY: The murder of Agamemnon is mentioned practically everywhere and by everybody in the *Odyssey*—it serves as a theme, counter to that of the poem we are listening to, for Agamemnon's return to treachery at the hands of a faithless and adulterous wife and her murderous lover is exactly the opposite of how the *Odyssey* turns out.

Pallas Athena pleads with Father Zeus to allow her to protect Odysseus, whose hardship can be traced to his crime against the sea-god Poseidon (Odysseus blinded Polyphemos, Poseidon's son—note that Odysseus acted in self-defense, an argument that has no bearing on the matter for the Greek mind). Zeus consents, as Poseidon is away on a visit to Africa, and the bringing home of Odysseus just might be accomplished before he returns.

The human action of the poem begins in Ithaka, where Penelope is being pestered daily by many suitors who assume that Odysseus is dead. She has kept them at bay for years, saying that she cannot consider marrying again until she has woven a shroud for her father-in-law, Laertes. At night she unravels what she has woven in the daytime. Her son, Telemakhos, has become increasingly fretful over the presence of the suitors, but is not mature enough to know how to deal with them.

Pallas Athena (disguised as an Ithakan named Mentes) comes to visit Telemakhos, and the problem of the suitors is brought to a crisis. She urges the twenty-year-old to take a stand, and even to set out in search of his father, for she gives him hope that he is still alive. She is so persuasive that Telemakhos guesses that a god (he does not know which) has come to take a hand in his affairs. The book ends with his going to bed full of hope and apprehension.

COMMENTARY: Note that the *Odyssey* begins where it will end, so that, in one sense, its form is circular. The picture of Ithaka in the first book is one in which Odysseus' absence is felt everywhere: by a faithful wife who cannot believe that Odysseus is dead, by a son who has a famous and heroic father whom he has never seen, and by the island at large, the kingdom of Odysseus. These bronze-age kings, called *basileís*, [singular, *basileus*] (basilas, basilews) were the equivalent of dukes in the Middle Ages, or perhaps large land owners, like a squire in England or a cattle-rancher in the United States. The king in our sense was more like a general of the armies of all the city states, and was called a *wánax* (Agamemnon, who led the Panhellenic expedition against Troy, was a *wánax*).

Note the psychological sureness with which Homer likes to create sly humor: Pallas Athena, in disguise, tells the same kind of cunning half-truths that will characterize Odysseus when he appears. Note that the suitors, when we first see them, are playing checkers—a game of strategy. What for them is an idle pastime is a reality for the heroic Odysseus, by whose carefully laid strategy they will perish at the end of the epic.

Homer handles young Telemakhos with superb realism: when he tries to assume authority as head of the house, he overdoes it, making empty threats, ordering his mother about, and filling himself with overconfidence for the council that will be a crashing failure on the morrow. (For a more careful discussion of the Telemakhos theme, see the CRITICAL ANALYSIS.)

Book II: Telemakhos Begins His Voyage

For the first time since Odysseus went away, the Ithakans are called to a public meeting in the marketplace. Telemakhos, inspired by Pallas Athena—and bravely present at his first assembly with two hunting dogs and his spear—calls the townspeople together. The first speech is by an elderly hero whose son sailed with Odysseus. He asks if Telemakhos has some news of their king's return.

Telemakhos replies that he knows no news of his father and wishes rather to denounce the suitors who are without honor. He explains that he is unable himself to make them behave with propriety, and asks them before the people to go about their courtship according to custom. Antinoös, the chief suitor, makes an angry and insulting reply, and insists that it is Telemakhos who is acting without propriety: he ought to send his mother back to her father, thus recognizing officially the strong suspicion that Odysseus will never return.

Telemakhos refuses, and in the heat of his anger prophesies unwittingly that Odysseus will return and kill all the suitors. As he speaks, two eagles appear above them and fight until they are bloody. The prophet (reader of omens in the behavior of birds) Halitherses, interprets this as a sign that Telemakhos is in the right and that evil days are in store for the suitors. He is laughed at, and Telemakhos is again urged to declare his mother eligible for marriage. He replies by saying that he is going in a ship with twenty men to search for his father. If

he learns that his father is indeed dead, he will comply with
their wishes.

Pallas Athena assumes the form of Mentor, an Ithakan, and
the ship is prepared. Telemakhos leaves word with his old
nurse Eurykleia, who prepares him for his journey, that Penelope is not to be told where he has gone unless she asks. So
with the goddess in disguise as his companion, he sets sail by
night for the port of Pylos.

COMMENTARY: Book II is one of the most romantic in the *Odyssey*, as it concludes with Telemakhos slipping
away on his adventure in the dark of night. This device
is as old as story-telling itself, and has become a permanent part of the adventure genre—the perilous setting
out of the innocent and inexperienced young hero.

The council meeting, too, is interesting for its
portrayal of the Greek social and religious awareness. It
shows us a number of characters, each of whom reflects
an attitude toward the problematic situation on the
island of Ithaka, as well as the impact of the Trojan war
on this remote, pastoral community. The prophet Halitherses is the first of many omen-readers in the epic—and,
of course, in all of Greek literature. Since the gods were
metamorphic and easily identified with certain animals,
the eagles that appear are, for Homer's listeners, a sign
of the presence of deity (the eagle was Zeus' bird; the
sparrow, Aphrodite's; the owl, Pallas Athena's, and so on);
the religion of the Greeks extended in its symbolism
throughout the whole fabric of creation.

Book III: Telemakhos at Pylos

Telemakhos' ship arrives at sandy Pylos at dawn (see
MAP, p. 5   ) when its people are gathered on the beach offering a sacrifice to Poseidon. The Ithakans are greeted cordially,
and Pallas Athena has the sly pleasure of saying a prayer to
herself, though ostensibly to her uncle Poseidon. Telemakhos
explains the reason for his visit. In answering him, old Nestor,

who was the oldest of the Greeks in the war and has seen three generations of men grow up (presumably he has lived to be about ninety), takes the occasion to tell of the homecomings of many of the great warriors. He is a good storyteller, and his accounts are vivid. He does not, however, know what happened to Odysseus, and suggests that Telemakhos go overland to Sparta to visit Menelaos, Agamemnon's brother and the husband of the reclaimed Helen.

COMMENTARY: Nestor figures in the *Odyssey* (as in the *Iliad*) as a patriarch. In the *Iliad* he is frequently a peace-maker in quarrels among the other leaders, and is skillful in offering compromises when there seems no way of reconciling two headstrong and differing opinions. Pallas Athena brings Telemakhos to him first not because he can say where Odysseus is, but because he is a magnificent old hero, a man of piety and strength and wisdom, and she wants Telemakhos to have had first-hand knowledge of him.

Nestor offers his son Peisistratos, the same age as Telemakhos, as a travelling companion. Mentor, who is, of course, Pallas Athena, declines to go, and disappears into thin air on her way back to the ships, revealing to all that a god has been present. After another great feast, Telemakhos and Peisistratos set out by chariot for the two-day journey inland to the "wheat-bearing plain" of Sparta.

COMMENTARY: Pylos, like Ithaka, is a seaport; except for its greater wealth it could not have been too different a society from that which Telemakhos already knew. Yet here were men who had seen his father ten years more recently than any Ithakan, and who had fought in the Trojan war. For the first time Telemakhos moves out into the great world where he has always known his father to be.

This visit, like the one to come in Sparta, is fairly static dramatically. But it is not unromantic; it has all the charm of visiting strange places and of seeing famous people: one of the major interests that kept ancient Greeks listening spellbound to the poem.

Pylos has been excavated in our time; there is an account in Leonard R. Palmer (see BIBLIOGRAPHY, p. 92) that explains why Pylos is called "sandy" (it seems to be the seaport for a Pylos of the Hills that is set further back from the sea). It was one of the great cities of the Mycenaean empire. Joseph Alsop's *From the Silent Earth* gives a summary of the archeology of the place and a history of its discovery.

Book IV: Telemakhos at Sparta

As at Pylos, Telemakhos arrives during a feast. But here he does not introduce himself: it was a Greek custom to be bathed and to eat before introductions. They are recognized by Menelaos as aristocrats and that is enough for him. Telemakhos' admiring the splendor of the palace,

> the flashing
> Bronze and silver and gold . . . the gleaming amber
> And ivory throughout these echoing halls . . .

causes Menelaos to speak of his travels:

> I have seen Cyprus, Phoenicia, and Egypt, and wandered
> Among Ethiopians, Sidonians, Erembi. So too
> I have been to Libya . . .

While they are talking, Helen appears—an electrifying moment for the Greek audience. This is the beautiful woman for whom the Trojan War was fought for ten years. For Telemakhos and Peisistratos, to see her was like having a history book come alive before their eyes. Homer's simile for her ("like Artemis") is ironic, for in her running away with the Trojan prince Paris (albeit urged by Aphrodite, goddess of love) she was the very opposite of the chaste Artemis, goddess of animals. Now, however, she is chastened and reformed: her past is forgiven if scarcely forgotten. She herself, in recognizing who Telemakhos must be, states:

> I look in wonderment
> At the young man here. Can any two people,
> Woman or man, look so alike as this young man
> Resembles Odysseus of the strong heart.
> This is clearly Telemakhos, who was still an infant
> When his father left for Troy to fight
> The awful battles for me, the bitch-eyed.

Telemakhos and Peisistratos introduce themselves, and Menelaos begins to tell of the war, even of Helen's cruel taunting of the men inside the Trojan Horse. As the stories go on, Helen slips a sleeping potion in their wine, so that they can forget the miseries evoked and sleep.

On the second day, Menelaos tells of his adventures in getting home. Like Odysseus, but in much less degree, he was thwarted in his return, and had to wrestle with the sea god, Proteus, god of metamorphosis, who lived in Egypt.

COMMENTARY: The account of how Eidothea, Proteus' daughter, heped Menelaos in his struggle, disguising him and his men as seals, is one of the strangest episodes in the *Odyssey*. The magic shape-shifter is known all over the world in myths, and Homer's is one of the best of these tales.

After telling of the fate of Aias (or Ajax) and of Agamemnon, Menelaos' brother, Menelaos eventually discloses that all he knows of Odysseus is that he was last heard of as a prisoner of the goddess Kalypso.

The story of Telemakhos at Sparta is interrupted, so that we can learn that back in Ithaka two things have happened. The suitors have discovered that Telemakhos has departed, and imagine that he is seeking help against them. They therefore rig a ship and sail out to murder him on his return around the cape. Penelope has discovered Telemakhos' absence also and weeps both in anger and in despair, that he has left secretly. The book ends ominously:

Midway between Ithaca and craggy Samos
Lies the rocky little island of Asteris, small to be sure
But having a harbor with a mouth on either side.
It was there the Achaeans lay waiting to ambush the Prince.

COMMENTARY: So ends "The Telemachiad." By beginning his
                  epic a few days before Odysseus' long-awaited
return, Homer manages to establish many things. He
creates a frame for his larger story, showing us the
world—in great detail—from which Odysseus has come
and to which he is about to return. He creates a sense
of urgency that Odysseus return soon, to avenge the
suitors, save his son, and bring order and peace to his
island. However strange and unnatural the adventures
of Odysseus (and they deal with witches, giants, cannibals, and monsters), we have been shown at the epic's
beginning a world that was as plain and everyday to the
Greeks as their own: a world of ships and farms, mothers
and sons and village people. So it is now dramatically
possible to change suddenly to the remotest part of the
world and meet Odysseus himself.

Book V: Kalypso's Enchanted Island

Zeus sends Hermes, the god of traveling, to go to Ogygia
and order Kalypso to give up Odysseus. It is decreed that Odysseus must go in a boat of his own building to Phaeacia, and that
the Phaeacians are to take him the rest of the way, and that
they are to give him gifts more costly than those he has lost.

COMMENTARY: With Book V begins the great center of the
                  poem that tells of Odysseus' adventures. It is
appropriate that it begins on Olympos, where the gods
again lay plans to bring Odysseus home.

Ogygia is a thick island forest, with many birds and
animals. Odysseus has been tempted for seven years to eat
ambrosia with Kalypso and thus become immortal. He has refused, though he is her lover, preferring to eat mortal food
and hoping for a return to his wife and child.

Hermes arrives, and Kalypso (not without trying to bargain) agrees to give up Odysseus and to help him build a ship.

Odysseus' first words in the epic are typical: he distrusts the goddess, and tries to see through her trick when she says that she is at last going to help him leave. The order in which they go about the departure seems characteristic of the heroic times that Homer is so careful to evoke: they eat, make love, and begin the four-day building of the boat. Once at sea, Odysseus sails for eighteen days before there is a mishap. His enemy Poseidon, returning from Africa, sees him in mid-ocean and promptly stirs up a great storm. One can hear the onomatopoetic onrush of the storm, the ominous rumble of the thunder in the Greek words:

ton dex aithiopon anion kreion enosichthor

The ship splinters and Odysseus is forced to swim. He would have drowned had not the sea nymph Leukothea given him her *kredemnon,* a sort of garment, possibly a veil or belt, that is magic and can be used as water-wings. Odysseus swims for two days and two nights until he comes to the coast of Phaeacia. His coming ashore is treacherous; he can find no safe place where the waves will not beat him against the rock cliffs. Finally he finds the mouth of a river. Here he swims in, gives thanks, and, utterly exhausted, makes a bed of leaves for himself, well hidden from he knows not what, and sleeps.

COMMENTARY: Note that this first adventure begins and ends in an enchanted island, for Phaeacia, like Ogygia, is meant to be under a magic spell. Phaeacia, we shall see, is a golden land, all graciousness and freedom and wealth. For the first time in twenty years, Odysseus is in an hospitable land.

The *Iliad's* predominating image is fire; Homer mentions it everywhere in the poem, working it into all the scenes as well as into the metaphors and similes. The *Odyssey,* on the other hand, is the epic of water; its largest symbol is the sea. The Greeks (unlike their neighbors to the southeast, the Phoenicians) had not mastered the sea, and in Homer's time regarded it as a treacherous place. "The unharvestable sea," Homer calls it in the first book of the *Odyssey*. And though its stock epithet is one of beauty ("the wine-dark or wine-faced sea") it is just as frequently the "unresting" sea—merciless and relentless. All of Odysseus' adventures are on or near the sea. Odysseus' enemy among the immortals is Poseidon, god of the sea. It is the sea, therefore, that calls for Odysseus' second greatest heroic virtue, endurance (the first is cleverness). This book is built entirely out of the two longest and toughest of Odysseus' endurances, his refusal to give in to the temptations of Kalypso, and the survival of the wreck of his raft. Homer chooses to show us Odysseus as a man of lasting strength, standing up to the limit of human endurance against the force of both physical power and despair.

At the same time the book is a bridge between two models of tranquillity and order. Kalypso's island is a model of supernatural order, a quiet paradise. Phaeacia, where he will be in the next book, is a model of human excellence in the art of living well. Neither is acceptable to Odysseus for the simple reason that neither is the home of his wife and son; one's own hearth was the Greek home—all one's loyalties were irrevocably there—and exile was the most terrible of fates.

Book VI: Nausikaa

While Odysseus lies asleep in his bed of leaves on the shore, Pallas Athena appears in a dream to Nausikaä, the young daughter of King Alkinoös. She appears as a friend of Nausikaa's, a girl her own age, and suggests that she ought to gather all the clothes that she will need for her wedding, take them to the clear springs near the sea, and wash them. Her parents are pleased when she tells them of her dream, and she is provided with a cart and a retinue of maidens.

COMMENTARY: This expedition, so charmingly primitive in its simplicity, is given the air of an excursion in the country and indicates the fairy-tale quality that Homer gives to his picture of the Phaeacians.

The girls do their washing, eat their lunch, and begin to play ball on the beach—one of the most beautiful evocations of youthful innocence in all of Classical literature. They are compared by Homer to the nymphs (tree and mountain spirits), and to the goddess of animals, Artemis (a chaste goddess).

Pallas sees to it that the ball gets out of hand and wakes Odysseus. Brine-encrusted and still weak with fatigue, he emerges from his hiding place and frightens all the girls except Nausikaä, whose royalty and sense of composure make her stand her ground with dignity, even though Odysseus looks like "a bold mountain lion."

Odysseus addresses Nausikaä graciously complimenting her on her beauty. He says—in a startling image—that she is the most beautiful thing he has ever seen except for a young palm tree on the island of Delos.

Nausikaä, too, makes a gracious and well-mannered speech and says that the laws of Zeus demand that all strangers be treated with courtesy. She invites him to follow her home to the palace, and Pallas Athena comes again to make Odysseus taller and handsomer before he accepts a suit of the newly washed clothes.

Nausikaä, young and bashful and sensitive about gossip (since it is known that she is soon to choose a husband from among her suitors), asks Odysseus to follow behind her at a distance. He is to wait awhile, to give her a start, in a grove of the goddess Athena, and here the book closes, with Odysseus praying to his protectress.

COMMENTARY: The tone of this book is achieved dramatically through its sharp contrast to one of the most harrowing of Odysseus' adventures. As the previous book showed us the virtue of *tlemosune* (the heroic endurance of extreme hardship), so this one shows us Odysseus as the cultivated man of *sophia* (intelligence, good breeding). The encounter of the naked Odysseus, modestly dressed in a leafy branch, and the aristocratic princess, the youngest of her family, has fascinated readers for two thousand years with the psychological clarity of its simple drama. The scattering of the alarmed girls, the charming picture of a princess doing the family wash, Nausikaä's falling in love with Odysseus, the contrast of the possessive goddess Kalypso and the very human Nausikaä—that these scenes should be so understandingly drawn by a poet who also described the battles of the *Iliad* has always been a source of wonder to Homer's readers.

Book VII: Odysseus at the Palace of King Alkinoös

The book opens with Odysseus praying in the poplar grove, sacred to Pallas Athena, where Nausikaä has asked him to linger until she reaches the palace. Nausikaä says nothing of Odysseus when she reaches the palace. Her brothers greet her, she goes to her room, and her old nurse, Eurymedousa, makes a fire for her and gives her her supper.

COMMENTARY: Elderly, loyal servants are a mark of order and long tradition for Homer, and he draws them with warmth and approval, usually telling something of their past, adding dimension and color to minor characters.

Odysseus, meanwhile, walks to the town where Pall...
Athena, disguised as a girl with a wine jug on her shoulder directs him to the palace. She also tells him, by way of casual gossip, something of the family's history, especially that of Queen Arete. Odysseus is impressed by the docks he passes on his way. The Phaeacians are a sea-faring people, though they have little contact with the rest of the world. They are, in fact, especially set aside by the gods as a happy, insular people whose prosperity and well-being are magically endowed —a divine compensation for many years of trouble in their homeland before they came to Phaeacia.

Homer's description of this beautiful land is consciously an evocation of fairyland, an enchanted place where the time is always spring. The palace, a place as richly designed as a Cretan city, is bronze, with golden doors swung on silver poles, and there is a blue enamel design around the top of the outside walls. Gold and silver mechanical dogs built by the divine smith Hephaistos guard the gates. Golden statues of athletes hold the torches that light up the great hall. Homer is equally interested in the opulence of the magic orchards around the palace and his poetry becomes especially rich when he describes the fruit that is always abundantly upon the trees:

Pear upon pear hangs ripe, apple upon apple,
And grapes bunch upon bunch, fig upon fig.

Odysseus marvels at this wealth, for the Greek love of material things was frank and open.

As Pallas Athena had made Odysseus invisible, so that he would not be questioned before he reached the palace, his entrance is of the dramatic kind that Homer liked. He is thus able to enter the palace and fall down and clasp Queen Arete's knees before anyone sees him. He pleads that he is a man of ill luck, given so many misfortunes by the gods that he cannot take the time to tell them. King Alkinoös generously gives him a seat of honor, feeds him, and shows the great sense of hospitality that Homer has demonstrated for us at Pylos and Sparta. Alkinoös promises to have Odysseus brought home, no matter how far he lives, the very next day.

COMMENTARY: This gracious hospitality provides a deep contrast to the hard adventure on the sea that has just passed, and to the seven years in which Odysseus was kept against his will upon Ogygia.

Book VIII: Games and the Singing of Epic Poetry

King Alkinoös calls an assembly of his citizens to announce that a ship must be prepared to take the stranger (whom they still do not know to be Odysseus) to his native land, however far. Their ships are magic, and their sailors are the finest in the world. Pallas Athena, disguised as a herald, goes about the town, urging people to the assembly.

COMMENTARY: Notice how this episode is like the preparation for Telemakhos' journey from Ithaka—by such 'rhyming' of scenes the epic poet achieves a deeper harmony in his design.

Once it has been decided that a crew of fifty-two men are to take Odysseus home in a black ship, the assembly moves to the palace, to drink and eat and hear the bard Demodokos (his name means "Esteemed by the People") sing.

COMMENTARY: This bard is a singer like Homer himself, and it has been supposed since Classical times that Homer was here inserting a self-portrait, hence the belief (for which there is no other evidence) that Homer was himself blind.

The bard, accompanying himself on the lyre (a twelve-string instrument mounted on ox horns and with a turtle shell for a sounding box), sings a narrative poem about Odysseus and Achilles. Odysseus is moved to tears by the song and Alkinoös, a man of tact and gracious manners, politely stops the recitation and suggests that they amuse themselves with games.

The most accomplished of the young Phaeacians come forward to wrestle, jump, throw the discus, and box. Their names make four lines of poetry.

COMMENTARY: The listing of names is an epic convention and would have been a delight for Homer's audience that we can easily miss.

> orto men Akroneös te kai Okyalos kai Elatreus
> Nauteus te Prymneus te kai Anchialos kai Eretmeus
> Ponteus te Proreus te, Thoön Anabesineös te
> Amphiolos th' wios Polyneou Tektonidaö

(ll. 111-114)

These names would have sounded wonderfully strange to a Greek, for they are like names in Dickens or in a fairy tale. Few translators have bothered to completely render them into English. They mean something like: Coxswain, Swiftsea, Pilot, Sailor, Skipper, Seaboard, Rower, Ocean, Captain, Fast, Launcher, Underweigh, Shiprich, Boatwright, Widesea (Euryalos, a few lines down), First Mate (Laodamas), Salt (Halios), and Boat-champion (Klytoneus).

Odysseus, still weary from his long swim, does not participate in the games until he is stung by an insult. He then hurls the discus further than any of the Phaeacians. Afterwards, he gives a hint as to who he might be. "Only Philoktetes was a better marksman with bow and arrow than I at Troy," he says. The Phaeacians are too well-bred to press him to tell his name.

To divert the stranger's attention from his annoyance over the insult, Alkinoös orders more music and poetry. This time nine young men dance while Demodokos recites the story of Ares (God of War) and Aphrodite (Goddess of Love). The song tells how they became lovers, and how Hephaistos (blacksmith of the gods and husband of Aphrodite) found them out and made a net of finely spun gold with which he bound them in the very act of love. He then calls the other gods to witness the wrong. The gods roar with laughter—'inextinguishable laughter.' So did the Phaeacians and Odysseus.

COMMENTARY: 'Homeric laughter' is clearly defined by the situation here. The laughable matter was that Ares was strong and handsome, while Hephaistos was lame and ugly; that Aphrodite had no self-control in matters of the heart; that the two were foolish enough to let themselves get caught; and that Hephaistos was hopping mad. The gods and the listeners are laughing at the delicious absurdity of the comedy, not at its salaciousness.

After the entertainment, the Phaeacians give Odysseus many rich gifts, which he promptly locks up against theft.

There is an exchange of compliments between Nausikaä and Odysseus, and between Demodokos and Odysseus, after which the hero asks to have the episode of the Trojan Horse sung to him from the cycle of Tales of the Trojan War which, as he has discovered, Demodokos has memorized. He listens with mixed feelings—delight and grief—to a recitation of history in which he played a major role, and which was the most daring enterprise of the war: the invasion of the city in a great wooden horse in which the best Greek warriors were hidden, and which the Trojans mistakenly and tragically thought was a sign of Greek retreat.

Odysseus' obvious personal response to Demodokos' singing has become by now a matter that Alkinoös cannot pass over in silence, and gently and graciously he asks Odysseus to tell his name and his history.

Book IX: Kikones, Eaters of the Lotos, the Cyclops

COMMENTARY: In this and the next three books Odysseus tells the Phaeacians of his wanderings and adventures.

Kikones   After introducing himself, at last, as "Odysseus, the son of Laertes, known among men and gods for the skilfull use of my mind," he takes up his story at his departure from Troy, with many men and ships and much booty. They make their first debarkation at Ismaros, land of the Kikones, where they burn the towns and take the women for themselves. Odysseus ordered a quick retreat from this hit-and-run raid (reminiscent of the Viking raids upon the English a thousand years later), but his men did not obey and they were caught by the counter-attacking Kikones, who killed six men in every ship. (In the *Iliad* the Kikones had been allies of Troy.)

They make their escape, only to run into a fierce storm that drives them off course for nine days.

The Eaters of the Lotos   They come to a land of sultry weather and tropical vegetation (presumably some North African port in the old Phoenician empire, possibly modern Algiers). Here the adventure is solely the temptation of a magic narcotic called *lotos*, a word that seems to mean "forgetfulness" to Homer. Odysseus must bring those of his men who eat the lotos back to the ship by force.

COMMENTARY: Note that three of the adventures which Odysseus narrates—Lotos Land, Circe's Island, and the Sirens—are concerned with the weakening of the will by a narcotic, soporific element. Odysseus is a man of determined will, and Homer keeps pitting this indomitable will against both brute force and the more seductive attack by the powers of lassitude, of lazy submissiveness.

The Cyclops The adventure of the giant, one-eyed Cyclops named Polyphemos (his name means either "Wordy" or "Famous") is one of the most elaborate. The wanderers come to Goat Island, in the bay of the Land of the Cyclops ("The Round Eyes"). Odysseus leads a foraging party to the mainland, enters the giant's cave, and is trapped there by the giant when he returns with his sheep. Polyphemos has Odysseus and his men at his mercy. Once his door, a great boulder, is in place, they cannot move it and escape even if they could sneak by him. They eventually get out, minus the men Polyphemos has eaten, by getting Polyphemos drunk on the strong wine they have with them, part of the loot from the Kikones. (It is the special brew of Maron, Son of Euanthes, which is to say "Sage Leaf, son of Prettyflower"—Greek wine, as it is today, was fragrant and strong).

Once Polyphemos is drunk, Odysseus takes a sharpened olive stake that he has heated white hot, and drives it into the giant's one eye. We can hear the onamotopoetic sizzle in the Greek:

> to gar awte sidarou ge kratos estin hos tou sidz ofthalmos
> (ll. 393-394)

The giant cries for help, and his neighbor giants come to aid him. But Odysseus has told Polyphemos that his name

is Nobody ("Outis"), and when the neighbors ask through the
stone door, "Who wrongs you?" he seems to say, "Nobody." So
the great stupid giant goes without help, and next morning he
follows his usual shepherd's routine. He opens his door and
sends his sheep out to pasture. Beneath the sheep cling Odysseus' men, holding onto the thick wool. It is one of the *Odyssey's*
moments of great tension (and one of Odysseus' cleverest tricks)
when the giant touches every sheep as it leaves.

Outside the cave, Odysseus and his men scurry to their
ships, and put to sea. In the bay, Odysseus shouts back his real
name to the angry giant, who retaliates by throwing huge rocks
at the ships, barely missing them.

Polyphemos then speaks to his father, the god Poseidon,
and asks that Odysseus never be allowed to return. It was this
adventure which had cost Odysseus a ten-year delay in his
return to Ithaka.

COMMENTARY: The first three adventures may have some basis in
                     fact. The Kikones are simply men defending their
homeland from the raiding Greeks. The Lotos Eaters are
probably a people in North Africa who used narcotics.
Polyphemos is an imaginary giant created by Homer
(as the French scholar Victor Bérard guesses in his
L'Odyssée d'Homère, Paris, 1931) to explain a point on
the map that he may have had as a clue to places where
Odysseus might have sailed. The map would have shown
an island, the modern Stromboli with its volcano, with
some annotation that its crater was a great burning eye,
that it threw rocks into the air, and made loud grumbling
noises. This was turned into "Polyphemos, the One-
Eyed" by Homer's imagination.

Odysseus' account of his first three adventures is
terse, sharp, and starkly clear. Historically (to step back
and look at the poem whole) we are listening to what
scholars believe to be, originally, a separate epic, "The
Wanderings of Odysseus." Homer would have inherited
the matter from another poet, and clearly the narration

has become beautifully compact in the telling. From a literary point of view we have an epic-within-an-epic. Note that Odysseus is in the same relation to the Phaeacians as Homer to his audience. We can guess that the art of epic recitation was very old by Homer's time to have developed such subtleties. (See "Commentary" at the end of Book XII and CHART, p. 7, for the symmetrical pattern of the adventures).

Book X:
Aiolos the Wind God, the Laistrygonians, Circe the Witch

Book X, like IX, tells three adventures:

Aiolos   The voyagers come to the floating island of the god of the winds, Aiolos, a place of supernatural strangeness. The island is walled by bronze, and the god's six sons are married to his six daughters. The atmosphere is of the fragrance of flowers and the sound of flutes (wind instruments!). Here Odysseus and his men spend a month happy and contented. As a gift, Aiolos gives Odysseus a bag of winds to use as he will in directing his ship.

COMMENTARY: This adventure hinges on the lack of wisdom in Odysseus' men—who were called fools in the very first ten lines of the poem.

The ship is in sight of Ithaka ("we could see men minding the watch-fires"—shepherds guarding their flocks from wolves) when the sailors, out of greedy curiosity, open the bag of winds while Odysseus is asleep. A great storm ensues, and they are blown all the way back to Aiolos' island. Aiolos is furious with them, and denounces Odysseus as a man of bad luck, and refuses to allow him to land. He is, Aiolos, says, "a man whom the happy gods hate."

The Laistrygonians   After a week's sailing they come to "the towering town of King Lamos, the Laistrygonian city of Telepylos." The Laistrygonians are a huge, ugly, cannibalistic people. They fall upon Odysseus' men with rocks (an ambush from the top of cliffs) and cause such confusion that Odysseus escapes with but one ship. The rest of his men are killed and eaten.

Circe   A single ship, its men weeping, arrives at the mysterious island of Aiaia. This episode is carefully built up, so that its strange nature is slowly and dramatically revealed. They land and mourn their lost companions for two days. On the morning of the third day Odysseus goes off by himself. He sees smoke coming from a house, but thinks it better for the men to eat before they explore the island, so he shoots a stag, and the rest of the day is spent in eating and sleeping. The next morning, Odysseus divides the men into two groups, one to explore, the other to guard the ship. The scouting party comes to a great palace, and the men are invited in by a beautiful woman named Circe (She-hawk), given a drink, and become swine. One man, Eurylokhos, escapes and brings the news to Odysseus. A god, Hermes (disguised as a shepherd), gives Odysseus a magic drug, the flower *moly,* that will protect him from Circe, and thus he is able to approach Circe, drink her potion, and be immune to the shape-shifting magic. He forces her to return his men to human form, becomes her lover, and spends a year with Circe and her nymphs. When Odysseus decides that he must continue his journey, he learns the most distressing news of all: he must, before he can return, descend into the world of Hades, King of the Dead, to learn from the old prophet Teiresias how to get home.

COMMENTARY: As we approach the exact center of the epic,
                     the next book, the tone of the poem subtly changes. All the adventures have suggested a world of dangers and peculiar modes of life unknown to Homer's audience, but the island of Circe takes us close to the world of the imagination where the natural and the unnatural are so woven together that all things are confused. Bestial and human life are equated in the fantasy. Time stands still. Circe is both benevolent and evil. Her nymphs are supernatural, yet they accept human lovers. Homer is suggesting that ambiguous half-light world that all men are aware of in myths and dreams, the edge of

human consciousness that we shall probably never fully explain. And he is carefully preparing us to hear of the world of the spirits beyond life, the ghost kingdom of the dead.

Book XI: King Hades and Queen Persephone

COMMENTARY: It has been guessed by scholars that this part of the epic is the oldest story that Homer has collected for his use, for some of the earliest of Middle Eastern myths concern a hazardous journey to the underworld (Tablet XII of The Gilgamesh Epic, for instance).

The exact details of how one sails to the kingdom of Hades are mysteriously smoothed over. Homer says that the entrance is in the land of the Kimmerians, near the edge of the earth, a land of constant fog. On the shores of this dark land they come to "the place of which Circe had spoken."

To talk to the shades of the dead, Odysseus had been instructed to make a little pit in the ground and fill it with sheep's blood, so that the dead could sip and have strength to talk. This he does, and ironically the first ghost is that of one of his own sailors, Elpenor, who had fallen and broken his neck when they were leaving Circe's palace.

Next comes the ghost of Odysseus' mother, Antikleia, who he did not know was dead. Yet he does not let her sip of the blood, for he must keep strictly to his instructions: he must hear Teiresias before any other.

Teiresias, a great prophet when he was alive (he was King Oedipos' seer in Thebes, as we learn in Sophocles' play), is now the sole ghost whose mental powers are as lively as they were on earth: this was a gift from Persephone, Queen of the Dead.

Teiresias explains to Odysseus that he will have trouble returning because he has blinded Poseidon's son Polyphemos. There will be further trouble if his men harm any of the cattle

of the Sun God, Helios Hyperion, on the island of Thrinakia.
He also prophesies that Odysseus will return to Ithaka "lonely,
late, and unhappy," and that he will find trouble there that he
must correct. He further tells him that he shall not die until he
has made a journey so far inland that the people have never
heard of ships or salt (the exact sign will be someone's mistak-
ing his oar for a winnowing fan).

The prophecy over, Odysseus speaks with his mother's
ghost. She tells him of Penelope's sorrow, and of his father's hard
old age, and of her own quiet death, which she says was brought
on by grief over his absence.

> But longing
> For you, for your quick mind and gentle heart—
> That surely took my honey-sweet life away.

Pitifully Odysseus attempts to embrace his mother, but she is
appearance only, without substance.

COMMENTARY: Next Odysseus sees the heroic mothers and
                grandmothers of Greek history; something is told
of each and the passage has been a source for many com-
pilers of myths and writers of tragedies. (The plot of
Sophocles' Oepidos plays, for instance, is reminiscent of
these lines; indications are that Homer was familiar with
an older or contemporary epic of the Theban Cycle,
which Sophocles later made use of.)

Then he is allowed to see the ghosts of the heroes who
fell at Troy: Achilles, Aias, and others. Next he sees those men
who must suffer for their sins: Tantalos and Sisyphos. He sees
Herakles, who speaks to him of his similar life of hardships, and
of his treacherous voyage to Hades. Odysseus would have stayed
longer in order to meet other heroes, but suddenly thousands of
ghosts appear, and he and his men quickly leave.

COMMENTARY: The Hades episode deepens the epic in its seri-
                ousness: the fact of death is always present in
the poem, but here it is brought to focus. As the adventures put the poem in contact with space (far lands,

great distances upon the sea), so this episode puts it in contact with time, the past and the future. No book of the *Odyssey* is more moving in its dramatic encounters: the accidental death of the uncautious Elpenor and his pitiful plea for a proper burial, the surprise and grief of Antikleia's presence, the ghostly solemnity of the prophet Teiresias, the matriarchal dignity of the 'great Greek women, together with their tragic stories or their proud status as the mothers of heroes, the ominous presence of the warriors and heroes, to remind Odysseus that he, too, no matter how loved of the gods or how cunning, will someday be among them. The last hero he sees is the one he is most like, Herakles.

Book XII: Sirenes, Skylla and Kharybdis, and Helios' Cattle

Odysseus and his men return to Circe's island, as instructed, and bury the luckless Elpenor, whose ghost they had seen in Hades' kingdom. Then Circe gives them more instructions and warnings. She advises them to choose the route of Skylla and Kharybdis instead of that of the Wandering Rocks (two rocks that clap together without warning when a ship is trying to sail between them). She tells them how to avoid the temptations of the Sirenes, and the dangers of harming the cattle of Helios Hyperion (a warning already made by Teiresias). They set out.

The Sirenes The Sirenes are beautiful sea-nymphs (though many Greek pictures of them show them as part woman, part sea-hawk) whose voices are irresistible. Odysseus puts wax in his sailors' ears, so that they cannot hear, and has himself tied to the mast, so that he can hear but cannot respond. For, as Circe has told them, the Sirenes eat the men whom they entice to their islands. Odysseus had expected their song to be a sexual temptation; they are subtler than that, and their beautiful song is all flattery of Odysseus and his warlike bravery, together with the promise that they are all-knowing, and can tell him anything he wants to know. He is indeed tempted to "linger awhile" with them, but he can do nothing about it, and they sail out of earshot.

Skylla and Kharybdis   Skylla is a six headed, loathsome, man-
                         eating monster who lives in a hole on the
side of a sheer cliff. The strait through which they must sail
flows just under her lair. One may avoid getting near to her
side of the strait by sailing on the other side, but here there is a
whirlpool caused by the sea-monster Kharybdis, who sucks the
water down and spews it up again: alternately a maelstrom
(such as the one that so fascinated Edgar Allan Poe that he
wrote three stories about it) and a twisting water-spout. To
keep his men from panicking, Odysseus does not tell them his
strategy. They skirt the whirlpool, placing themselves just under
the cave of Skylla. In a moment of sheer terror for the sailors,
she eats six of Odysseus' men—"they looked like fishes flopping
on a hook as she took them up."

The Cattle of   Next they come to the island called Thrinakia
Helios Hyperion   (Sicily, which fits the name, "three-corner-
                     ed"). They know they must not eat the cattle
there. Yet an awful month-long storm keeps them there and,
fearing starvation, the men disobey Odysseus while he is praying to the gods, and slay the cattle. The hides that have been
skinned away begin to crawl and the very meat bellows while
they eat it. They leave in fear and haste. A storm comes up,
wrecks the ship, and kills all the men but Odysseus, who holds
onto part of the splintered ship, survives a passage through
Kharybdis' whirlpool (he holds onto a fig tree while the water
sucks from beneath him, and floats on when it spews up again).
His tale comes full circle when he tells how he reached the island of Ogygia, where Kalypso the goddess rescued him and
kept him for seven years.

Thus he has told his adventures to the Phaeacians, and
is ready when dawn comes to be taken to Ithaka in the magic
ships of Phaeacia.

COMMENTARY: Abstinence, a nerve of steel, piety: these are
                   the heroic qualities with which Odysseus had to
answer the seductive songs of the Sirenes, the treacherous
passage between the monster Skylla and the fatal whirlpool Kharybdis, and the holy cattle of Helios the Sun
God.

Note that Odysseus is the kind of man who did not want to miss the experience of the Sirenes' song; especially note that he is genuinely tempted. In all of his adventures he moves to the brink of disaster, and saves himself by the skin of his teeth.

In the opening lines of the *Odyssey*, we are told that Odysseus' men perish because they are fools. The height of folly for the Greek mind was impiety, presuming to act against the will of the gods. And their impiety is punished with as strange a response of the gods as we are shown in the epic: the ghostly lowing and supernatural movement of the cattle's hides.

Book XIII: The Return

COMMENTARY: Scholars surmise that the epic was originally thought of as having three parts: the *Telemachiad* (Books I-IV), the *Nekuia* (nekwe-a) (Books VI-XII) or Wanderings and Adventures, with the Descent to Hades as the most important, and the *Nostos* (Books XIII-XXIV), or The Return. In looking at the unity of the poem, we see that the Return, even though it is an independent episode in itself, is the continuation of The Telemachiad (which closed with the cliff-hanging incident of the suitors waiting to waylay and murder Telemakhos), and is as well the last and greatest of the adventures.

Book XIII begins to move more slowly than previous ones, for it is the first step toward the restoration of Odysseus to his throne. The Phaeacians bring him to Ithaka with great speed, and put him ashore in a remote cove sacred to nymphs. He is asleep when he is laid with his treasure in the cove—a state of affairs befitting the magic nature of the Phaeacians. They, however, have their ship turned to stone just as they reach Phaeacia again: fulfilling the old prophecy that someday they would be punished by Poseidon for bringing a stranger home. The island itself is ringed with mountains, forever cut off from the rest of mankind.

When Odysseus awakes, Pallas Athena has enchanted his
eyes, so that he does not recognize his own island. She herself
appears in the shape of a shepherd, asking who he is. Out of
cunning caution, he tells an elaborate lie. He is, he says, a Cretan
(notorious liars, if we are to believe ancient tradition) who has
wandered far, got lost, and been put ashore by Phoenicians.

Athena is amused by this lie, and reveals herself and
laughs with Odysseus. They two, she says, are the cunning ones,
she among the gods, he among mortal men. Surprisingly, Odysseus complains that he has missed her help while he was having
his hardest times. She explains that she has helped him all she
can, short of drawing down yet more wrath from her uncle,
Poseidon. But now, she says, the important thing is to plot a
way to avenge himself against the suitors.

She withers his body to that of an old man, gives him
rags to wear, and counsels him to move secretly and cautiously
toward his revenge. They hide his great treasure in the nymphs'
cave, and Odysseus goes inland.

COMMENTARY: At the very center of the epic Odysseus has
                          ended his account of the adventures. Now, at
the beginning of XIII, he is ready to be taken to Ithaka
by the Phaeacians. At this point the epic re-commences
the plotline it was following through Book VIII—the adventures have been a digression. Homer heightens the
magic of the Phaeacians by having their ships operate by
supernatural force (they move as swiftly as a hawk).

               Note that Odysseus is landed, asleep (as if under
a spell, as no doubt he is), in a sacred grove. Even when
he awakes, he is placed under enchantment by the gods,
so that he cannot recognize his native land without the
help of Pallas Athena. Odysseus is a man of pragmatic
character; he is acutely intelligent, practical, cautious. Yet
Homer likes to place Odysseus in strange environments
(the contrast is far greater than it would be with a character who enjoyed mystery). The dimension of enchantment ends in this book. The rest of the epic will be in a

real, everyday world. Note the severe transition from the sacred grove to the swineherd's hut.

When Pallas Athena discloses herself (with a lady-like laugh) to Odysseus, she says:

> hoonek epatas essi kai angkhinoös kai ekhefron because you are courteous, shrewd, and prudent.
> (l. 332)

This is an important line, for the goddess of the intelligence is characterizing Odysseus to his face. *Epatas*: gentle, courteous, deferential, with good manners. *Angkhinoös*: intelligent, flexible of mind, alert. *Ekhefron*: prudent, sensible, wise, a good strategist.

Book XIV: Odysseus and the Swineherd Eumaios

Odysseus walks until he comes to the hut and sties of his own swineherd Eumaios, a faithful old peasant. The dogs set upon him and have to be called off. Homer gives a full and rich description of the swineherd and his hut and all its sows and boars. But most of all he is interested in showing us the character of Eumaios, a faithful servant who misses Odysseus, who feels as keenly as Telemakhos the ravages of the selfish and insolent suitors. The scene is as delicious to Odysseus as to us, for we are aware of who Odysseus is, and can appreciate the unconscious ironies of everything the simple swineherd says.

Odysseus maintains his disguise, and tells another long lie—a kind of miniature Odyssey—about his wanderings. He has known Odysseus at Troy, and prophesies the return of Odysseus within the month. This is too much for the old swineherd to believe. He openly dismisses Odysseus' talk as fabrication, but nevertheless finds him an entertaining old beggar, and gives him a cloak in which to sleep. It is a stormy night. This disguised return of the King is a great dramatic device, and few story-tellers have managed to imagine so fine a detail as the hero cozily asleep on his own property for the first time in twenty years, among the pigs, the night ominously foreshadowing the reckoning to come for the whole island.

COMMENTARY: Homer's concept of the order of society is humanistic. Eumaios represents the humblest station in the hierarchy, and yet he is chosen to speak for the sense of disorder felt by the whole society. Many social critics judge a society by its lowest orders, that is, whether the health of the society extends to all of its members. Homer is, in effect, showing us the excellence of Odysseus' rule when he takes such minute care to introduce Eumaios as a major character in the epic. And Odysseus is repaid for his wise rule by the hospitable care Eumaios offers.

Homer's original audience evidently took great delight in the elaborate tales that Odysseus was capable of telling. For the second time Odysseus casts himself as a Cretan (a traditional convention—a people noted for their unwillingness to tell the truth in the first account of anything, especially before a stranger). Yet Odysseus, in all his lies, is essentially conveying a truth, like a man speaking in riddles. His mask is partially transparent. And all the tales he tells from this point forward are subtle ways of building up hope in his return.

Book XV: Telemakhos' Return to Ithaka

This book falls into three parts: Telemakhos' trip from Sparta to Pylos and out to sea, homeward bound; Eumaios' account of his life, told to Odysseus; and Telemakhos' arrival in Ithaka, having safely eluded the suitors waiting to kill him.

The book opens with Pallas Athena coming to Sparta, where she finds Telemakhos and Peisistratos (Nestor's son) asleep. She advises Telemakhos to return home immediately, to protect his mother, and further warns him of the suitors in ambush, telling him how to avoid them. Telemakhos leaves early the next morning, laden with gifts, including an embroidered gown made by Helen herself, to give to his bride. As they are preparing to leave, an eagle swoops down and carries off a goose. Helen reads this omen as a sure sign that Odysseus is soon to return and drive off the suitors.

COMMENTARY: This omen is balanced at the end of the book, when Telemakhos lands on Ithaka: a hawk catches a dove in mid-air.

Telemakhos and Peisistratos retrace their former trip, but when they reach Pylos, Telemakhos goes immediately to his ship, knowing that old Nestor will delay him with well-meant hospitality. As he is about to cast off, he is approached by the prophet Theoklymenos, fleeing avengers. Telemakhos gives him passage on his ship. While they sail toward Ithaka, Homer shows us Odysseus and Eumaios in the swineherd's hut.

Odysseus asks Eumaios of his past, and learns that Eumaios was kidnapped from his native island as a child by his Phoenician nurse, who, as a slave, sought escape back to her homeland. She died at sea, and the Phoenicians sold the little Eumaios to Laertes, Odysseus' father. He was raised as a lad alongside Odysseus' older sister, Ktimene. But when she was married to a husband in Samos, he was sent to the farms to be a swineherd. We learn in the tale that he is a prince.

Meanwhile, toward dawn, Telemakhos arrives and disembarks at a landing away from the town, so as to go directly to the swineherd, as Pallas had directed. He turns the prophet Theoklymenos over to his friend Peiraios.

COMMENTARY: Twice in this book which is devoted mainly to the action of getting Telemakhos home again, we are told tales of the lost and the homeless: the kidnapped Eumaios, the fleeing Theoklymenos. These tales thus reinforce the overall theme of the *Odyssey*. A society with pirates and slavery was bound to generate personal tragedies such as these; told here, they enliven the dangerous possibility that Odysseus and Telemakhos might easily have perished far from home.

Book XVI: Telemakhos Meets His Father

COMMENTARY: This book is set first in the swineherd's hut, where Telemakhos arrives; then at the palace of Odysseus, where we see an exchange of sharp words between Penelope and the suitors; and again at the swineherd's hut. Its major action is the meeting of Telemakhos and Odysseus, but its real dramatic business is to build up more suspense toward the resolution of the plot.

Telemakhos arrives from his excursion to Pylos and Sparta and is greeted warmly by Eumaios. He speaks with the old beggar, expressing his frustration and helplessness. Once the swineherd goes off to tell Penelope that Telemakhos has returned, Pallas Athena arrives and changes Odysseus back to his proper form. Telemakhos realizes that the great moment has actually come: his father has returned. They weep without restraint, "like sea-hawks or taloned eagles, when farmers take their young from the nest." Then they plot how best to avenge themselves against the suitors. Telemakhos is skeptical that they can kill them, pointing out that there are 108 of them, not counting six valets, two servants, the herald, and the bard. Odysseus says that they will have Zeus and Pallas on their side.

While they talk, the listener is taken to the palace, where Eumaios arrives simultaneously with the herald from Telemakhos' ship, so that Penelope learns from two sources that her son is safely back. The suitors are chagrined that they have failed to kill Telemakhos, and again plot his death. Just then, while they are at such dark talk, Penelope comes to reprove them, reminding Antinoös that his father's life was once saved by Odysseus, and that his insolent waste of her property is doubly sinful on that account. Eurymakhos, another suitor, makes a deceitful speech to Penelope, assuring her that Telemakhos is his dearest friend.

The book ends with a short scene in which Eumaios returns to his hut. Since he is still to be kept in ignorance of the beggar's identity, Odysseus is turned back to his disguised self.

COMMENTARY: Note that this book is a skilfull study in appearance and reality, and that the disguises are of two sorts, those of the suitors (where an appearance of benevolence hides treachery) and that of Odysseus (where a false identity keeps secret a carefully laid plot to effect justice, when the time is ripe). The epic will move toward its end with many recognition scenes, of which the meeting of Telemakhos and Odysseus is the first.

Book XVII: The Begger Odysseus in His Own Palace

COMMENTARY: This book falls into two sections, each ending with a scene of the suitors feasting and wasting Odysseus' goods. The book opens in the swineherd's hut, from which Telemakhos first goes, then, later, Odysseus (in his beggar's disguise) and Eumaios. Once they are all converged at the palace, we are shown the suitors at their worst insolence.

Telemakhos is greeted by his old nurse Eurykleia and then by Penelope. He tells of his meetings with Nestor and Menelaos. The prophet whom he brought to Ithaka with him is introduced to Penelope, and prophesies that even now Odysseus is on Ithaka. Over the years Penelope has heard so many rumors that she pays little attention to his soothsaying, or to the hints dropped by Telemakhos. This scene is brought to a conclusion with a glance at the suitors at play and at dinner.

Meanwhile, Odysseus and Eumaios have set out for the palace. On the way they are made fun of, and even kicked, by the goatherd Melantheus, who is in the pay of the suitors and comes out daily to select their meat from the herds.

When they draw near the palace, Odysseus pretends to guess that it must be the house of the renowned Odysseus (the swineherd is still in the dark as to who he is). His old dog Argos, lying on a dung hill, recognizes Odysseus' voice but dies for joy before he can inadvertently betray his master.

Odysseus gives yet another lying account of himself,

emphasizing the fact that he was once rich, too, before his fortunes changed. He infuriates Antinoös, who throws a footstool at him.

Penelope, always willing to talk with wanderers who claim to have seen Odysseus, calls the old beggar to her quarters. He sends word, however, that he will come later.

COMMENTARY: The dramatic impact of this book is to set the scene for Odysseus' eventual disclosure—the better prepared for, the more startling it will be when it comes. Practically every action, every speech, is rendered ironic by Odysseus' disguised presence. Note how every word takes on a double significance. We see the suitors unwittingly writing their death warrant. We see Eumaios and Penelope living in a world of hope when what they hope for has already been fulfilled.

Book XVIII: The Begger Critic

COMMENTARY: In this book Homer is concerned entirely with creating scene after scene in which Odysseus is allowed to criticize the suitors' misbehavior, and to accumulate evidence against them to justify their deaths when the reckoning comes.

The book opens with an ominous forewarning of what is to come. A pesky beggar named Iros turns up, quarrels with Odysseus, and gets into a fight with him. The suitors, of course, are delighted, for what is more entertaining to loiterers than a fist fight? With a single blow Odysseus dislocates Iros' neck and sends him bleeding from the yard.

Odysseus takes this occasion to talk at length out of the side of his mouth. Only Amphinomos, a suitor, takes the hints for what they are worth, and is filled with dread.

Penelope makes another appearance, to chide the suitors. This time she has some effect, for it is suggested that the suitors bring her gifts, which they do (ironically, for they are about to give their necks as well).

The rest of the book is given over to scenes, as in the previous one, where Odysseus sees with his own eyes the extent of the insult which his household has had to bear. Melantho, a whorish serving maid, insults him, as does Eurymakhos, in a long and sharp exchange of hateful words. But Odysseus gives as good as he takes.

COMMENTARY: It is the sensitivity of the Greek toward due honor and respect that generates all of the action of Book XVIII. Insolence was the mark of the deficiency of an order. Here we are shown brawling in what ought to be the privacy of a house; we see a stranger mistreated (a sin against Zeus); we see mother and son in disagreement; we see prostitution among the female servants; we see the overbearing intrusion of the suitors into practically every detail of the household's order.

Homer, by showing us an entire book devoted to the topsy-turvy state of Odysseus' palace, builds up Odysseus' anger as well as our sense of the justice Odysseus is going to effect.

Note that this book is very close to the literary technique of the modern novel: it is realistic, unheroic, and is concerned with the everyday world. If the beggar were not an Odysseus in disguise, however, the episode would lack point for the Greek audience, except as the picture of a disorderly household.

Book XIX: Odysseus, Penelope, and Eurykleia

COMMENTARY: Around the central dramatic shock of the recognition of Odysseus by his old nurse Eurykleia, Homer here builds an intimate scene in which the disguised Odysseus and Penelope talk: he to his faithful wife in whom he finds no disappointment whatsoever; she, to a beggar who has seen her husband but who is helpless (without revealing himself) to alleviate her despair.

The book opens with a piece of strategy: Odysseus has the weapons removed from the banquet hall (so they will not be available to the suitors when he strikes).

Then begins the long scene between Odysseus and Penelope. Melantho, the sluttish maid, is again reviling Odysseus when Penelope reproves her and orders a chair for Odysseus. Again he spins a lying tale of who he is, where he has been, and how he has seen Odysseus, of whom he gives an accurate description in order to convince Penelope that he is correct.

Eurykleia is called in to bathe Odysseus. She at once recognizes on his thigh the scar he got when he was a boy, and is about to reveal the secret when Odysseus puts his hand over her mouth and whispers that she must wait. At this point (while Penelope notices nothing) Homer weaves in the pastoral account of the boar hunt that caused the scar, of boyish days with Grandfather Autolykos (Grandfather Wolf), and of how Odysseus got his name.

Then in a passage of great poetry, Penelope, almost as if she were thinking out loud, and certainly as if she were unburdening her heart for the first time in years (she has found a listener in the beggar to whom she can speak), compares herself to the nightingale in the myth of Philomela, tells a prophetic dream, and speaks of dreams in general, explaining about the two gates of ivory and horn from which lying and true dreams come. She then announces that she is going to set a task for the suitors (there is some suspicion that she knows it is impossible): namely, that they string Odysseus' bow (something that only Odysseus has been known to do) and shoot an arrow so straight that it goes through the handle-holes of twelve axe-blades set in a row.

COMMENTARY: With what admiration Odysseus must have listened to all of this! The character of Penelope was first built up by brief glimpses of her, but here her character emerges strong and well rounded, a character befitting and matching that of her cunning and formidable husband.

Book XIX provides a framework for three of the *Odyssey's* most magnificent passages: Odysseus' description of himself to Penelope, the tale of how Odysseus came by his scar, and Penelope's account of her prophetic dream. Each is a digression to recover parts of the past that must be known at this point in the narrative, yet each is self-contained, a complete poem in itself. Nor is their organization a mere stringing together. They are dramatically unified by Eurykleia's recognition of Odysseus' scar and her having to keep the secret from Penelope —no easy feat for an old woman whose entire life is devoted to the happiness of her mistress.

Autolykos, Odysseus' maternal grandfather, is called "accomplished," "a man of great enterprise" with whom, Homer adds, no man could hope to compete in the matter of stealing or telling lies. It is clear that (however sly a smile the singer might have assumed at these words) Homer is praising Autolykos, for he explains that he was blessed especially by Hermes the god, himself no backward practitioner of the arts of lying and thieving. Professional piracy lasted well into the twentieth century in Greece (and the rest of the Mediterranean countries), and has thus a "noble" tradition.

The device of Odysseus' scar allows one of many passages that have established Homer as the masterful poet and true father of Western literature. In itself it is a barbaric detail that helps, as well as being a neat functional device for the plot, to define further Odysseus' character. More than this, it is a distinguishing characteristic of Homer's art that at any moment the action might reverse or shift and flow in another direction as well, as here into the childhood world of Odysseus: his grandfather, a mountain landscape with a boar-hunt, and the primitive, pastoral roots from which his family sprang. The scar also shows us the devotion of Eurykleia and her relationship with Odysseus—a relationship founded when Odysseus was a boy and she a middle-aged woman charged with keeping him out of mischief. We see at once that there is deep understanding between them. They have a faith in each other's shrewdness; they can communicate with a glance. It is clear that Odysseus, the boy, had studied and admired this sly, sharp-eyed old woman, and had learned a part of his own craftiness from her. The disclosure of a secret is one of the never-failing ploys by which fiction pleases, but few storytellers have managed a scene like this, at once tense with drama, rich with disclosures of character, and also a moment for reaching back in time to tell a story.

Book XX: Signs and Prayers

COMMENTARY: Homer opens and closes the book on the note of drunken laughter: first of the undisciplined maidservants; later of the suitors.

Penelope prays to Artemis, the chaste goddess, to send her death, as she can no longer expect to have the stamina to withstand the disgrace and indignity of her situation.

Odysseus also prays, first to Pallas Athena, and asks her what safety from an eternal blood feud he would have even if he were able to slay all the suitors. She reminds him that men often place their faith in men; how much more faith should he have when his friend is a goddess? Then Odysseus prays to Zeus, asking his guidance. For answer he gets a thunderclap (Zeus' usual signal of approval to mankind) and overhears a patient, faithful servant complaining to herself in the kitchen, a woman overworked by the constant demands of the suitors. He takes this to be a sign, as well, and knows that it is the will of the gods that he slay the suitors.

The next day is the Feast of Apollo, and Eumaios and Philoitios come to town. (Philoitios, as faithful and adoring a servant as Eumaios, will come in handy at the great moment). Odysseus is again taunted by Melantheus the goatherd. A man named Ktesippos also taunts him, and throws a cow's foot at him. At the height of the riotous feast, which is even more drunken than usual in honor of the holiday, the suitors demand that Telemakhos (whom they have been plotting again to kill, although their omens have been against such a move) go and order his mother to choose a husband from among them. At this moment Pallas Athena causes them all to giggle and laugh hysterically: she has cast a spell on them, so that they seem to be gibbering idiots. This is a terrible and moving scene (it is like the cruel caricatures of the Spanish artist Goya, or like the mediaeval pictures of fools by the shipload), and in its midst the prophet Theoklymenos has a vision of blood and slaughter. At the close of the book, Homer compares the vast quantities of meat on the banquet tables to the dead bodies of the feasters soon to strew the floor of the same room.

COMMENTARY: Note that Odysseus in his anger at the suitors remembers the time he was trapped in the Cyclops' cave; Penelope prays to the goddess Artemis. And for his reliance on his own self-confidence, Odysseus is comforted by Athena. In this parallel we can see how Greek religion was a crystalization of centuries of thought about the nature of life. Artemis is the goddess of chastity; that is, of the well-behaved woman. Athena is the goddess of intelligence. Penelope turns to the idea of her personal integrity; Odysseus, to the strategy of the battle he must fight.

With this book Homer completes his case against the suitors. Their misbehavior is reduced to a disgusting and impious riotousness, so that Odysseus' task begins to seem like one of the labors of Herakles—to purge the land of a plague.

Book XXI: The Bow of Odysseus

The day has come for the contest of the axe-blades. Not only must the archer be a straight shot, but he must first be able to string the powerful bow of Odysseus. (We are told its history and why it was not taken to the war.) Homer draws a

scene worthy of the tense occasion. The first contender fails;
he is Leiodes, son of Chaodes, Oynops, a man skilled in omens.
While the other suitors are futilely trying to string the great
bow, Odysseus calls Eumaios and Philoitios aside and reveals
himself to them, and gives them instructions whereby he is to
have a chance at stringing the bow.

The suitors are in disgrace: none can bend the bow. They
rationalize that the next day might be more propitious, and
argue that some god, Apollo the Archer perhaps, keeps them
from having the strength to string it. Odysseus begs to have a
try and is roundly laughed at. Penelope orders that he be given
a chance. Telemakhos, who knows what is about to happen,
sends his mother to her part of the palace.

Philoitios and Eumaios bar the doors from outside.

Odysseus, in a delicious moment of triumph, strings the
bow with ease, and twangs it. It sounds like the voice of a
swallow in springtime. Against what dead silence that twang
sounded!

The wooers, we are told, grew ill and pale. Odysseus
easily sends an arrow through the aligned axe-blades.

COMMENTARY: For dramatic staging, this book, full of sudden
                  surprises, ranks high in Homer's epic. The book
ends with a kind of snap. The trap has been sprung; the
quarry, a hundred-sixteen men, is caught.

No book in the *Odyssey* better illustrates Homer's
dramatic skill. Revenge, says a Mediterranean proverb,
is a dish best served cold, that is, surprise is the psycho-
logically important element of revenge. Homer adds his
own flavoring to the moment: revenge not only comes
when least expected, but also from an unsuspected source.
Odysseus' disguise has already created many fascinating
moments (with Eumaios, Penelope, the suitors) and here
it achieves equal if not greater intensity.

Book XXII: The Slaying of the Suitors

Odysseus strips himself naked (so that they can witness the transformation from beggar's body to that of the heroically built Odysseus, and so that he can put on the armor that Telemakhos will bring). He first shoots Antinoös, through the neck. At first the men think that the shot is a tragic accident. Then as he refits the string with another arrow, they realize that they are to be executed. They cry for mercy. Odysseus calls them dogs in return, insulters of his wife, wasters of his goods, and corruptors of his servants. Eurymakhos pleads that the culprit is already dead, that it was Antinoös who led them astray and kept them acting like despoilers and that they will repay what they used, and add gifts as well. Odysseus answers him with angry words and an arrow that strikes him in the nipple of his breast and is driven through his liver.

The battle begins in earnest—Telemakhos has brought armor, and the four men, with spears and arrows, begin the slaughter.

Melantheus slips through the door that Telemakhos has foolishly left open, and grabs armor for the suitors. On his next trip he is caught by Eumaios and tied to a board upside-down from the ceiling.

Pallas Athena comes to join Odysseus, now as Mentor, now as a swallow in the beams.

The slaughter is total. Only the bard and the herald are spared. The twelve faithless maidservants are brought in to wash the blood from the floors and walls and then they are hanged. Melantheus is horribly mutilated and flung out into the courtyard with the corpses. The old nurse Eurykleia is the first to enter the scene of slaughter. She rejoices, but Odysseus forbids her to be glad of death; he orders a fire to be built, so that the room can be fumigated with sulphur.

COMMENTARY: Only the awful battle scenes in the *Iliad* are as pitiful and accurate as these descriptions of death. From our later point of view, it is an utterly uncivilized mode of behavior, but the time Homer describes was one of strictest honor, and Odysseus was repaying insult with death.

Such a scene as this, where the hero is in full command and achieves a victory, was called by the Greeks an *aristeia*, a full display of power and skill. Throughout the *Iliad* the heroes are given their moments of *aristeia*— the great showing forth of heroic grandeur. It is in keeping with the spirit of the *Odyssey* that Odysseus shares his heroism with Telemakhos and the faithful servants.

Book XXIII: Husband and Wife Together

Eurykleia, the old nurse, runs to tell Penelope that Odysseus is indeed home. Penelope, however, will not believe. Her disappointment over the years has been too deep to erase in a single moment of surprise. She cautiously sits apart from Odysseus and waits until he can give some foolproof clue to his identity. He asks slyly if someone has moved his bed (he and Penelope alone know that one post of their bed is a tree still rooted in the earth below). This intimate detail convinces Penelope and she accepts her lord in tears.

Odysseus warns everyone that their trouble is only beginning. As soon as the town knows of the slaughter, they will come to avenge their sons. Odysseus has already had the musicians play loud music, to fool the people into thinking that a great feast is going on rather than the removal of corpses. He plans to make a stand in the hills, at his father's house, the first thing in the morning. Meanwhile, they are safe for the night.

Odysseus and Penelope go to bed and he tells her a short version of his wanderings. They make love, and sleep.

In the morning, hidden by Pallas Athena, the men slip out of the palace and head for the hill country.

COMMENTARY: The dramatic tension of this book has two
               sources: the recognition of Odysseus by Penel-
ope, and the fact that at any moment the kinsmen of the
slain suitors may arrive to begin a blood feud.

Nowhere in the epic is Homer the dramatist so
evident as in the recognition scene. We expect—especially
modern readers—a joyous reunion. What we see is a
battle of wits, the toughness of Penelope's integrity pitted
against Odysseus' wily mind.

It is typical of Homer's art that the meeting of
Odysseus and Penelope happens before the plot relaxes
its suspense. A lesser story-teller might have reversed the
two last books, and described Odysseus and Penelope
together when all their worries were over. When the
tension is gone, the story is over. The epic proceeds (in
the next book) only four lines beyond the assurance that
there will be no feud; that is, beyond what the whole
poem has moved toward, the restoration of order that was
destroyed twenty years before.

The opening of the last book of the epic invites
us to compare Odysseus' return with that of Agamemnon
(whose wife had killed him). The contrast is not between
Odysseus and Agamemnon but between the faithless
Klytaimnestra and the faithful Penelope. For this reason
the twenty-third book is focused upon Penelope. Her
happiness is the important emotion; her redemption from
loneliness and the rewarding of her patience become more
significant than the primitive justice of Odysseus's slaying the suitors.

Book XXIV: Peace

COMMENTARY: The theme of Aigisthos, seducer of Klytaimnes-
               tra and slayer of Agamemnon, is brought to a
fullness (and conclusion) at the beginning of this last
book of the epic.

The scene is in the Land of the Dead. The suitors arrive. Agamemnon questions them, and gets a full reply. His response is to praise the faithful Penelope at the expense of his adulterous wife. The story of Agamemnon, as Homer has suggested throughout the epic, is the exact opposite of that of Odysseus.

Odysseus and his men reach the farm of his father Laertes, who is in his gardening clothes. Even here and even now Odysseus sees fit to tell another lying tale, for the joy of disclosing himself to his father after he's fooled him. He must also prove his identity to his father, as with Penelope.

The situation is desperate. Old Laertes gets into armor for the first time in many years. The tiny band stands to fight off the townspeople, who are now climbing to the edge of the farm. The two groups face each other. Laertes kills Eupeithes, and Odysseus and Telemakhos begin to fight with swords and spears, but Pallas Athena, again disguised as Mentor, comes between them. Her voice is divine, and is the voice of intelligent reason. She demands that the feud stop here and now. Zeus sends down a thunderbolt to indicate that his authority, too, is behind her words. Both sides see the wisdom of halting a blood feud that might last generations. With the blessing of the goddess of intelligence upon them, they part in harmony.

COMMENTARY: The largest theme that runs through the epic is that of the control of brute violence by the force of intellect and reason. It is the poem of peace and the reasonable ordering of life, as the *Iliad* is the poem of force and war. No quieter ending could be imagined for the poem than a sudden, god-ordained cessation of the violence that had been building up for over half of the poem. The most that Odysseus could think of in his cunning was that he and his family must flee their island, and even that would not have insured tranquillity for them.

So, too, the poem performs a great trope in its movement from the remote enchanted island of Ogygia, tropical and strange, to the orchards and vineyards of old

Laertes. For the Greek mind the poem ends in a triumph of sanity and civilized life. The island king has come home. He brought with him the spirit of the cruel war itself; in a sense the last battle of the Trojan War was fought in Odysseus' banquet hall. But peace and harmony are a gift from the gods, that the tormented story of Odysseus might be ended in a vision of the good life which has eluded all Greeks for twenty years.

CRITICAL ANALYSIS

The Literary Achievement

Homer's Style   Every age finds different qualities to admire in Homer—this would seem to be the mark of great literature, that it endures as its beauty and truth are adaptable to the tastes of each generation. In the twentieth century, for example, Ezra Pound has celebrated the *realism* in Homer (see "Commentary" to Book XVIII, p. 59): the slaying of the suitors is intimate to its smallest gory detail, chariots and ships are described with great technical accuracy. The frequently sustained irony of the paradoxical epithet (the "wise" Telemachus, the "noisy" dogs in situations where they may not be so); the poet's wry, occasionally off-slant humor (see discussion of the laughter of the gods at Hephaistos' "catch" in his golden net, Book VII); the sudden and horrible shock of, in the midst of gaiety and merry-making, the neck of Antinoös neatly skewered by Odysseus' first arrow (Book XXII)—these show Homer, the poet of antiquity, to have skillfully handled those facets of literary art which so preoccupy the "modern" poets.

Matthew Arnold, the English critic (1822-1888), found four qualities in Homer's style: rapidity, a plainness and directness in the evolution of his thought, a plainness and directness in the substance of his thought, and nobility.

By nobility, Arnold meant several things. One is Homer's command of the emotions he evokes. He is never at a loss with a human emotion, and describes with perfect understanding such divergent emotions as Nausikaä's girlish love for Odysseus, Odysseus' temper fit when he is insulted at the Phaeacian games, the monstrous rage of the Cyclops, the dainty eeriness of all Circe's actions (notice how she comes to Elpenor's funeral with wine and food, paying no more attention to what's going on than if Odysseus' men were polishing their armor), the pitiful scene of Odysseus' attempting to embrace his mother's ghost in Hades, the rustic charm of old Laertes' country clothes, described with care.

Homer is never embarrassed by any human emotion. Nowhere in Homer can we find him disapproving of a person acting according to his own nature.

Homer always speaks with an easy fluidity. He is neither wasteful nor stingy with words. His culture was verbal (the Greeks are still a people who love to talk, especially to tell stories in an orderly and unhurried way, taking their time with all the details). He does not point to anything; he shows. Epic poetry was meant to teach as well as to entertain, and Homer's mode of teaching was to establish resemblances, hence the use of *simile* when he wants us to see exactly. The Homeric simile takes something familiar (a farmer recoiling from a snake) and puts it beside something we have not seen (a soldier recoiling from a sudden ambush). We see the two together, and understand the one by means of the other.

The similes can be elaborate (as when Odysseus approaching Nausikaä and her friends is compared to a mountain lion disturbed in its den) or terse and epigrammatic:

> Even as the generations of leaves, so are also those of men
> (*Iliad, VI. 146*)

Greek is a language in which a poet can achieve extraordinary effects, and Homer has many unforgettable lines in which he has made the words speak with great eloquence. For example:

> dana de klang-ga genet argire-oy-o bi-oy-o
> (*Iliad, I, l. 49*)

The line describes Apollo shooting an arrow from his bronze bow: familiar with the Greek or not, the listener can hear the clang of the released string, and its quivering. Homer is a master of onomatopeia (imitative sound) and uses it to powerful effect; few translators have succeeded in carrying this quality across the language barrier.

Homer is always concrete: he talks in terms of things rather than abstractions. It was, however, the nature of his world that he assigned human qualities to objects. A sword was made of "pitiless bronze."

Homer's ideal of directness and swiftness can be seen in his approval of sharp, eloquent speech—"winged words," by which he apparently alludes to the feathers at the back of the arrow's shaft (or the swift flight of the swallow or the hawk).

Form   Though the wanderings of Odysseus occupy ten years
        (three years of adventures and seven with the nymph Kalypso), the action of the epic occupies forty days (thirty-three days from the setting out of Telemakhos to the setting out of Odysseus from Phaeacia; the second half of the poem, from Odysseus' landing on Ithaka to the peace treaty at Laertes' farm, takes a week). Note the symmetry of 3 and 7. The thirty-three days fall thus:

1—Athena comes to Ithaka to counsel Telemakhos.

2—Telemakhos sets out.

3—Telemakhos lands at Pylos.

4—Telemakhos travels from Pylos to Pherai, midway to Sparta.

5—Telemakhos' arrival in Sparta.

6—Telemakhos' stay in Sparta.

7—Hermes is sent to Ogygia.

8 to 11—Odysseus and Kalypso build a raft.

12 to 28—Odysseus is at sea on his raft.

29 to 31—Poseidon wrecks the raft and Odysseus must swim.

32—Nausikaä takes Odysseus to the palace.

33—Odysseus tells his adventures to the Phaeacians.
34 to 40—Odysseus is on Ithaka at last; he slays the suitors.

Such clear form is the result of conscious artistry, although the material Homer was re-working had been sung for many years before he made an epic of it. The student who finds himself interested in the beauty of the poem's symmetry should know that all the art of Homer's period tends toward geometric, balanced lines and areas. The more we look at the form of the *Odyssey*, the more we find to admire in its symmetries. Note, for instance, that the beginning is devoted to Telemakhos, the end to Penelope, and the center to Odysseus, though his presence, actual or psychological, is over the entire poem. The student can find many other symmetries in the adventures (in their nature, in their sequence).

The Wanderer Theme

Homer is the western world's first and perhaps greatest writer. If we look at his peculiar ability to satisfy practically all tastes, we will see that what we're talking about is Homer's wonderfully generous mind. He lived in an age that, as far as we know, was much changed from the world he describes in his epics. His world was commercial and bureaucratic. So in a sense he was describing a world (the times of Mycenae, Knossos, and Pylos as world powers) in a slightly transformed way. This does not make his great generosity any the less real or sincere.

By generosity we mean the view whereby everything and everybody has its place in a world that the poet accepts. He never condemns the actions that are native to a place or a people. The Aiolians, for instance, are incestuous (and very happy, Homer adds); the Laistrygonians have always been and probably always will be cannibals; that's the affair of the Laistrygonians and the gods. Nothing is ever to be changed: Circe is a witch; no missionary will ever make her anything else! Homer is a very moral man, a religious man if you will, and yet it was the nature of his religion to accept the world in its large diversity. He is not shocked by any of the world's behavior. We might note, however, that he sees the world as a matter of everything remaining in its native habitat. The Cyclops are terrible but they stay at home. Odysseus makes a clean break from every adventure. We must assume that Kalypso (who loved Odysseus and wanted to keep him forever) could not leave Ogygia; nor Circe, Aiaia. Except for Odysseus, Homer's characters are as rooted as trees. Such a view of things also enforces the great nostalgia that keeps Odysseus homeward bound.

If Homer was dispassionate, he knew what the nature of things was. In a sense, all the action of the *Odyssey* is toward getting a husband back to his wife and son, a king back to his kingdom. Odysseus, the most famous of wanderers, had nothing of the wanderer about him. He was simply lost and detained.

Think how impossible it would be today to describe the emotions and motivation of the hero of the *Odyssey*. We would helplessly be involved in noting that Odysseus is childishly selfish, hypersensitive, greedy, cruel, adulterous, impious, scheming, and murderous. Odysseus will not have changed, only the capacity of a culture to understand him. All the bad words just mentioned melt into thin air when we turn to Homer's generous eyes. The selfishness is the ordinary Greek desire to excel in wealth and in honor; the hypersensitiveness is healthy suspicion (as when Odysseus locks his presents in a box and whips a foolproof knot around the clasp in front of the Phaeacian donors, as if they might steal back what they just gave him). The greed is motivated by its opposite, poverty, which to the Greek was shameful. Homer accepts the full animal potential of the human being as a norm of behavior. Odysseus is, to modern eyes, as amoral as the lion to which he is frequently compared. At the same time he is a civilized man, with a poet's eye (he compares Nausikaä to a sapling growing by the altar of Apollo in Delos). He sees all and forgets nothing; his curiosity is as alive as his animal awareness of the dangers around him. Pallas Athena is pleased to bracket herself with him, noting that he is the cleverest and slyest of mortals, as she of the immortals. It is significant that his first words in the epic question the veracity of a goddess.

The Telemakhos Theme

In the second book of the *Iliad*, when Odysseus in a council of the Argive leaders is rebuking Thersites, he refers to himself as "Telemakhos' father" (line 260)—"may I never again be called the father of Telemakhos if I don't rip off your clothes and beat you out of the camp." Again, in the fourth book of the *Iliad* (line 354), Odysseus says to Agamemnon before an encounter with the enemy that soon everyone will see "the father of Telemakhos engaged in close in-fighting with the Trojan champions."

It is the destiny of Odysseus' family that each father has one son only. The opening of the epic with an account of Telemakhos is therefore not a mere literary device but a deliberate focus on the continuity of Odysseus in his son. If Telemakhos is not a son worthy of his father, the entire effort of Odysseus to return is undermined. Odysseus' triumph in his home-coming depends on Penelope's having been a faithful wife, on his servants having remained loyal (the best of them have), but most of all on Telemakhos' being found worthy of carrying on the heroic virtues of his father. The drama of the epic's beginning is in the psychological clarity with which we are shown an adolescent *almost* worthy of his father. He is doubtful of his prowess, he overdoes his rebuke of the suitors, he is, in short, between boyhood and maturity.

Modern writers and critics have especially admired this portrait of the young Greek finding his way in growing up by longing to find his lost father. The American novelist Thomas Wolfe embodied the theme in his first novel, *Look Homeward, Angel* (1929) and again in his long novel about maturation, *Of Time and the River* (1935); and in both works he invites the reader to think of his hero as "the young Telemachus." The theme of the growing son and a lost father (frequently a spiritual father rather than an actual one) has become a dominant theme in modern literature. We can see it in Mark Twain's *Huckleberry Finn* (which is an Odyssey along a river, with adventures that are symbolically comparable to those of Homer's epic), in Melville's *Moby-Dick* (where the hero's name, Ishmael, recalls a Biblical son exiled from his father).

Around the turn of the century we can see that many writers became more interested in the theme of Telemakhos' spiritual plight than in the character of Odysseus. For example: Samuel Butler's *The Way of All Flesh* (a novel about a son who rejects his real father and searches for a set of values that will symbolize for him an ideal father), James Joyce's *A Portrait of the Artist as a Young Man* (a novel that alludes throughout to the psychological connections between father and son, as does the sequel to it, *Ulysses,* an extremely complex re-telling of the Odyssey in modern terms). In our own time J. D. Salinger's *The Catcher in the Rye* re-states the theme of Telemakhos, and William Golding's *The Lord of the Flies* is the same theme seen in reverse, showing that children without fathers (that is, without a clear direction and continuity) lose civilization altogether and revert to a primitive bestiality.

Note that the *Odyssey* begins and ends with Telemakhos, and that in contrasting the two pictures of him, we have a way of seeing one of the sharpest meanings of the poem. At the beginning he is unsure of himself, indecisive, and filled with fearful hope. At the end of the poem he is standing with his father and his grandfather. He has fought beside his father to kill the suitors and is ready to fight again. He has grown up.

Homer and the Epic in the Literary Tradition

The great Roman epic, the *Aeneid* of Vergil, is a conscious imitation of Homer. Vergil is a more compact artist, and uses twelve books only, six of which are in imitation of the *Odyssey* (I-VI), six in imitation of the *Iliad* (VII-XII). That is, by Vergil's age (just before the beginning of the modern era) it was assumed that Homer was the greatest epic poet and therefore the only model to imitate. However, Vergil's hero, Aeneas, is nothing like the interesting, complex person Odysseus.

In the Latin Middle Ages the text of Homer was not

available to Europeans (though it was very much read in the Byzantine Empire). Dante did not read Homer.

By the time of the Renaissance, we find a whole new world to discover and read Homer. (The figure of Odysseus managed to live apart from the text of the poem; he appears, for instance, in Dante's *Inferno*, in Chaucer, and in many other references).

Using Homer as his model, the Portuguese poet, Camoens, wrote an epic poem about Vasco da Gama. In the years after the Renaissance, Homer was more translated than imitated, though we ought to remember that such seemingly non-Homeric works as Milton's *Paradise Lost* were inspired both in language and form by Homer.

The modern poem closest to Homer in feeling and scope is Charles M. Doughty's *The Dawn in Britain* (1906).

The Greek poet, Nikos Kazantzakis (best known for his novel *Zorba the Greek*), wrote a sequel to the *Odyssey* in 33,333 lines, an engaging and extremely interesting poem that is basically philosophical. The wide-eyed wise innocence that characterizes the Homeric gaze at the world died when Homer died.

But the spirit of Homer has never been more alive than in the twentieth century. James Joyce's novel *Ulysses* (perhaps the greatest of the twentieth century) is based on the *Odyssey* in a clever, symbolic way. (His Odysseus is a middle-class citizen; the adventures are the distractions of civilization. Aiolos, the wind god, for instance, is a newspaper office in Joyce's novel; Circe's house is a brothel, and so on.)

Ezra Pound's long epic poem *The Cantos* is another modern work based on the *Odyssey*, with modern equivalents for the adventures.

William Saroyan's novel (and movie script) *The Human Comedy* is also based on the *Odyssey*, again with a re-interpretation of the adventures in modern terms.

And the qualities of Odysseus keep cropping up in all literatures: Robinson Crusoe is a kind of Ôdysseus, as is Sherlock Holmes and Tarzan of the Apes.

The *Odyssey* is thus a classic because it (a) is of permanent interest, (b) has not dated (or faded or remained in our attention merely as a quaint curiosity) for two thousand years.

The importance of the *Odyssey* can be understood in several ways:

1. Its portrayal of human life in the Greek Bronze Age is unique. Its contemporary, the *Iliad,* shows life in the hardships of the military. The *Odyssey* presents a range of great width in its picture of Greek life, from shepherds to kings.

2. Homer's skill with language (which the non-Greek-reader must see through the translator's eyes) has been equalled only by Shakespeare and James Joyce, and perhaps not yet surpassed.

3. The creation of the figure of Odysseus ranks in its way with the highest achievements of Greek art, with the Parthenon in architecture, the art of philosophical inspection in Plato.

4. The *Odyssey* (along with the *Iliad*) is the work without which we cannot proceed to real knowledge of the literature of Europe.

CHARACTER ANALYSIS

Homer, as Aristotle says, depicts "men in action." We learn the character of Homer's people from the way they act. He never introduces them (as many novelists do), nor does he ever explain their personalities. A character may have an epithet attached to him ("Wily Odysseus," "Godlike Telemakhos") but this is almost an honorific title conferred by long traditions of story-telling, and the epithets are sometimes used ironically, when the character is doing something the opposite of what his epithet implies. Homer's characters are always complex of character, and they are never static. Notice, for instance, that Telemakhos at the beginning of the epic is unsure of himself; at the end he stands beside his father and helps slay the suitors. Notice the surprise in Penelope's character when she refuses to recognize Odysseus.

Telemakhos   His name, meaning "Far from Battle," was given because he was born when the male generation of his parents were going off to the Trojan War. But the name proves to be ironic, for the epic ends with Telemakhos taking part in two battles. Homer's portrait of this young man is charming and complex. When we first see him, he is a mother's boy, a bit pampered; moreover, he is the son of a world-famous father—a difficult reputation to live up to. Pallas Athena comes to him with a purported reason, to give him fame by having him search for his father (though she knows he cannot find him); in fact, her purpose is to have him grow up a little, to confront him with what he has never seen, men who, like his father, have fought at Troy and moved in the big world. His role in the epic is to portray a young man growing up in Bronze Age Greece. We last see him standing within the accurate order of the clan of Odysseus, when Grandfather Laertes, Odysseus, and Telemakhos, all in armor, all defending the ancestral estate, receive the blessing of Pallas Athena and of Zeus.

Penelope   Her name is apparently not Greek, and seems to be the name of a water-fowl of some sort. She is literature's archetype of the faithful wife and is thus the opposite of Helen, that romantic woman whose shining presence haunts both the *Iliad* and the *Odyssey*. Penelope is as crafty as her husband, and as long-suffering in her own way. She is vividly characterized in the first four books, but not until the second half of the epic do we see her contending with the insufferable suitors, with her own courage and sorrow. She is a pious woman, stalwart, brave. On the island of Ogygia, Odysseus refuses immortality for her.

Antinoos   With Eurymakhos, the most important of the suitors. He is irresponsible, insolent (Homer's constant word for him), and arrogant (all in view of the fact that Odysseus had once saved his father's life). He is the first of the suitors to die.

Eurykleia   Odysseus' and Telemakhos' old nurse. Her name means "Far-Famed." She is a portrait of faithfulness, devotion, and love. Only Gustave Flaubert has drawn a more eloquent picture of a servant, in his story called "A Simple Heart." Eurykleia manages to connive with Telemakhos (so that he can make a secret get-away on his journey) without disobeying Penelope. She has two great moments in the epic, aside from the minor scenes where she is the helpmeet of the family: one is her recognition of Odysseus (by a scar on his thigh) when she is bathing him on his return disguised as a beggar; the other is her dance of triumph after the suitors are slain—a wonderfully primitive response to a gory scene, and Odysseus has to reprove her.

Eumaios   Odysseus' swineherd. Though he is a faithful servant, we learn that he is noble-born, and we hear him tell the story of his kidnapping. Homer shows us a picture of country life with great feeling for Eumaios' rustic simplicity—a detail that gives reality to our understanding of what Odysseus' kingdom was like.

Laertes   Odysseus' father. We do not meet him until the last book, though he has been mentioned all along. He is elderly and has retired to a farm in the hills, the scene of the epic's close. He is characterized by his clothes and by his passion for gardening. His having to put on armor at the last is a master-stroke of drama.

Antikleia   Odysseus' mother, she appears in Hades, a ghost. She lost interest in life when she feared that Odysseus would never return, and this had hastened her death. We see her only as a figure of great pathos.

Melantheus   The disloyal swineherd contrasts with the loyal
                Eumaios, above; Homer may want to have Me-
lantheus typical of all those servants in the palace who were
quick to take advantage of the suitors' control. It is important to
see that, in Melantheus' situation, there are few men who
would not have done the same. It *did* appear that Odysseus was
dead and would never return. It would be foolish not to serve the
suitors and gain their favor as one would evidently soon be master of the palace. Such behavior is obviously to Melantheus'
personal advantage, but it is nevertheless without honor. In the
end he is tortured and killed with as brutal a scene as appears
anywhere in Homer.

Menelaos   The aristocrat from a richer, more ornate culture
                than Ithaka. Sparta (or Lacedaimon, as it was also
called) was not at this time the highly disciplined military city
state that it was to become in the fifth century. Homer describes
Menelaos' palace as if it were oriental. We gather from Menelaos'
account of his adventures that he is of Odysseus' calibre, but
with less chance to exercise his mettle.

Helen   The wife of Menelaos, the lover of Paris, the woman
                for whose recovery the Trojan War was fought. She
makes but two appearances in the *Odyssey*, but her presence
is grand and her story, like that of Klytaimnestra, is remembered
throughout the epic. That she appears only as a chastened and
modest wife is in keeping with the tone of the poem.

Nestor   Homer's portrait of Nestor at home is of a pious, el-
                derly king. He is full of proverbs and worldly wisdom,
a giver of advice. There is a touch of humor in Telemakhos'
avoiding him on the return trip, disclosing that the garrulous old
man is a bore to the young man.

Nausikaa   One of the most charming girls in all literature.
                Her falling in love with Odysseus (a school-girl
crush) is a beautiful stroke of characterization. She is like
Miranda in Shakespeare's *The Tempest*, who knows only the
calm order of her ideal country. In Odysseus she is seeing the
outside world for the first time. Her poise before Odysseus on

the beach is an example of the gracious self-control that the Greeks so valued.

Odysseus   Homer's other great hero, Achilles, was a man of skill and strength. Odysseus is the man of cunning, of thought. The *Iliad* is a poem about force; the *Odyssey* is a poem about the triumph of the mind over force. Hence Odysseus is, in the largest sense, a man of the intellect, though he is as strong and as tough as Achilles. He is "long-suffering," that is, patient, and the nature of the trials set him by the gods required that he be heroically patient. In every adventure we can trace his and his men's survival to his forethought, his prudence, or his ability to think his way out.

SUGGESTED QUESTIONS AND ANSWERS

1. In what sense were the suitors arrogant?

Suggestion: Collect Penelope's, Telemakhos', and the townsfolk's spoken objections. Consider all the reasons (there are several) why the suitors weren't simply dismissed.

2. What advantage does Homer's way of telling the story (beginning toward its chronological end and working backward, and then going swiftly forward again) have over a straightforward account?

Suggestion: There is (as all good novelists know) the duty of the story-teller to keep alive all the possibilities for surprise. Note the effect of withholding Odysseus' appearance until the fifth book. Also note how Homer is usually telling two plot-lines at once.

3. In what ways does Telemakhos mature?

Suggestion: Note the kinds of experience he has and indicate what kinds of emotional maturity he gains.

4. One of the great themes of the epic is that of homecoming. In what ways, other than the final scene, does Homer enforce this theme?

Suggestion: Consider the happiness of Telemakhos' return; the peaceful scenes showing the returned Nestor and Menelaos, and note how Odysseus returns to his family and faithful servants one by one, beginning with the humblest and ending with his father.

5. *The mark of a great poet is the breadth of his understandstanding. List as many different types of human beings as you can that Homer depicts.*

Suggestion: Think in categories: foreign and domestic; excellent and deplorable; magic and natural; humble and aristocratic; well-mannered and ill-mannered, and so on.

6. *Most of the English poets you have read place a great deal of importance on natural beauty (landscape, flowers, and such). What was Homer's attitude toward nature?*

Suggestion: Homer is explicit about the land: Ithaka is rocky and goat-pasturing; Lacedaimon is grassy, hilly, and horse-pasturing. Note that he names trees and plants (look at the descriptions of Ogygia, Aiaia, and Kimmeria). He gives the color of things (hair, the sea, the sky). His mind is oriented toward agriculture (you could draw an accurate picture of old Laertes' garden; all the plants are named.)

7. *In the first line of the epic we are told that Odysseus is "versatile of thought, never at a loss." List some of the ways in which Homer illustrates this.*

Suggestion: Look at the way Odysseus gets out of scrapes (Skylla and Kharybdis, the Cyclops, Circe) and especially at the carefully laid plan whereby the suitors perish.

8. *The Odyssey is a strange mixture of the primitive and the highly civilized. Give examples.*

Suggestion: The hospitality of the Phaeacians, the brutal slaying of the suitors, the cannibal Laistrygonians, the ceremonial giving of gifts, and so on.

9. *The Odyssey was composed to be heard, not read. List some details that indicate this.*

Suggestion: The repetitions of passages, the identifying epithets, the constant quotation of speech (giving the reciter the chance to be an actor as well). There are others.

10. *The Odyssey has always been admired for its humanistic qualities (that is, its reflection of an attitude that honors the sanctity of human lives). In what sense is Homer humanistic?*

Suggestion: His definition, by inference, of the family and the roles of each of its members (the good husband, good wife, good son—consider wherein the goodness lies). His relationship of god and man. Odysseus is pragmatic but not cruel, for the most part; the slaughter of the suitors is as much a cultural as a personal matter (consider the vendetta in Mediterranean history). His ideal for man is a well-ordered family on a well-ordered property.

11. *Discuss the Odyssey as a Romance.*

Romance is the literary form involving long and perilous journeys, accounts of strange and fabulous countries, adventures, and narrow escapes. Defoe's *Robinson Crusoe,* Stevenson's *Treasure Island,* and Spenser's *The Faerie Queene* are English romances. The hero of a romance is usually a traveller seeking for treasure or a person or country difficult to find. The plot of a romance follows the triumph of a courageous and skillful man over natural and supernatural forces. Consider the fact that we invariably read the *Odyssey* as a romance whether Homer and the Greeks thought of it, or not, as essentially romantic. The romantic qualities of the *Odyssey* can be seen most clearly in Odysseus' adventures, in the detailed picture of the land of the Phaiacians, and in the triumphant return home.

12. *Discuss the realism of the Odyssey.*

Aside from the psychological realism of character, Homer gives many scenes in which the everyday life of people is vividly depicted. Examples: old Laertes in his orchard (note his country clothing, his garden tools); Menelaos and Helen at dinner; Penelope weaving; Nestor talking to his guests; the games of the Phaiacians. There are many other examples.

13. Outline briefly the structure of the Odyssey.

There are three principle parts: (1) Telemakhos' search for his father, which establishes by implication the character of Odysseus and shows us other heroes of the Trojan War who, unlike Odysseus, have returned years before; (2) Odysseus' adventures, (3) the return.

14. Why do women play such an important part in the adventures?

Circe keeps Odysseus a year; Kalypso, seven years. Nausikaä, the Phaiacian princess, falls in love with Odysseus. The Sirenes tempt him to remain with them. These are all obstructions to Odysseus' return to his faithful wife Penelope. It is dramatically fitting that they be temptresses. They are in contrast to Penelope as well as to Pallas Athena, who protects Odysseus. The attention of the tempting women build up a context that establishes Odysseus' desirability as a husband (as the attention of the suitors establishes Penelope's desirability as a wife).

15. What qualities in Odysseus' character would have been most admired by the ancient Greek audience?

His endurance in hardship and his strategic skill. The word *Hero* in Greek meant first of all the power to protect one's native land (Theseus and Herakles are examples); that is, strength as a fighter and patriotism as a citizen. Odysseus (as can be seen in the *Iliad*) has these qualities; but he is also preeminent in the more personal heroic qualities of patience, determination, guile, and intrepidity.

16. What qualities in Odysseus' character have been most admired in modern times?

Since the Renaissance, Odysseus has become a symbol for the spirit of intelligent inquiry (as in Tennyson's "Ulysses"), of exploration, and of that daring forwardness of mind which has distinguished European and American scientific and technological advances in the last four hundred years. That is, Odysseus (like the mythological craftsman Daedalos) is a figure in ancient literature who seems to embody an attitude toward the world that we like to think of as our own.

17. Discuss the Odyssey as a poem of peace.

The *Iliad* has frequently been called the great poem of force. The *Odyssey* displays not war but an orderly peace as the best of life. The strategy of the epic's plot is to put in order again a disordered world. Odysseus the adventurer longs for the quiet of his home. The Trojan war, disastrous to the order and peace of Asia Minor, has also disordered Ithaka. Any disorder, Homer implies, disturbs the entire world. In the last scene of the epic Pallas Athena commands the Ithakans to be at peace with each other forever.

18. Discuss the importance of Kimmeria (the entrance to the house of Hades) and of Phaeacia.

The two adventures can be seen as extreme opposites. The one is the land of death, darkness and sterility; the other is the land of eternal springtime, brightness, and fertility. Both are in the realm of the supernatural. The one is the lowest; the other, the highest point of Odysseus' adventures. Yet they are alike in that each is necessary to Odysseus' finding his way home. He is guided to the one by Circe, the most sinister of the women in the epic; and to the other by Nausikaä, the most innocent.

19. Zeus says in the first book of the Odyssey that though men blame the gods, they are themselves the cause of their misfortunes. Is this justified by the action of the epic?

This is a difficult question to answer, for so much of the human infraction of divine law is brought about by dire necessity (for example, the eating of the cattle of Helios Hyperion, the blinding of the Cyclops). It is hard for modern readers to see how the suitors deserved death, or why so many of Odysseus' men had to die by violence (eaten by Skylla, for instance). Zeus' pronouncement is good Greek theology the logic of which depends on our thinking strictly in the terms of their religion, and that is all but impossible to do. It is clear that Odysseus saves himself by a pious regard for the laws of the gods, and that he is almost lost by his blinding of the Cyclops. We must understand Zeus to mean that the gods are not malevolent (unless sorely provoked), that they are forces which care for and protect mankind. But they are also forces that chastise his waywardness and insolence. Odysseus must cross the element—the sea—that belongs to the one god he has offended, so that Zeus' words are true enough for his troubles.

RESEARCH AREAS

1. The exact nature of Odysseus' heroism.

Suggestions: Correlate the adventures with what seems to be the Greek idea of endurance, bravery, cunning, and determination. Compare an adventure of action (the escape from Polyphemos) with one of patient endurance (Kalypso). Contrast Odysseus and Antinoös and Agamemnon. Is Odysseus' graciousness (as before Nausikaä and Queen Arete) part of the heroic ideal?

2. Homer's portrayal of Greek manners in regard to visits, the giving of gifts, providing the amenities.

Suggestions: Describe the accommodation of Telemakhos at Pylos and at Sparta. Note the dramatic contrast with the suitors' treatment of Odysseus in his own house.

3. Homer's use of the supernatural.

Suggestions: The gods and their actions were not supernatural to Homer or his audience. But the land of Phaeacia was (it is obviously an ideal country, a Utopia); and the islands of Ogygia and Aiaia.

4. Pallas Athena as a personified quality in mankind.

Suggestions: Try to see all the actions of Athena in the epic as matters which a modern (realistic) novelist would understand as either intellectual or psychological. Can all her actions be accounted for in modern terms?

5. *The appearance of the heroines and mothers of heroes in Hades.*

Suggestions: Look up their myths (Ovid's *Metamorphoses* is the best place to look, although an encyclopedia or a handbook of Greek myth will serve your purpose) and explain why Homer introduces these particular stories at just this place. You will find that there is a *thematic* answer (a satisfying of the artistic pattern). For example, if Odysseus' mother appears, it is a fitting occasion to bring on the mothers of other heroes, either for enrichment by duplication or by contrast. There are other possible answers: the nature of the history of Odysseus' world; the improvement of the human race by intercourse with the gods; the touching of human and divine life (which is what is happening when Odysseus goes down to Hades).

6. *The difference between the first and second half of the epic.*

Suggestions: Note that the first half is appropriate in our time to the moving picture; the second half to the stage. Note that the action of the first half is swift, but that the dramatic situation is lax (or subdued). In the second half the action slows, but the suspense and drama mount.

7. *The metaphors.*

Suggestions: Collect a half dozen or so and analyze them to see how the Greek audience better understood the action described by the use of the accompanying metaphor. Are the metaphors gratuitious, or do they subtly add a dimension to our understanding? Are some of them comic?

8. *The interpolated stories.*

Suggestions: Note that these stories, usually inserted as digressions in the midst of the flow of action or narration, are devices by which the past is added to the present, and by which Homer can deepen the time-sense of his narrative. Examine, for instance, the story of Odysseus and the boar (told while old Eurykleia, the nurse, is washing him). Or the story of Eumaios (a little novel in itself). Or the adventures of Menelaos.

9. *The archeological reality of Homer's world.*

Suggestions: Note that both the Bible and the Greek classics were interpreted in the nineteenth century as mythological accounts about people and places that never were, but which were essentially true (that is, poetically true). The twentieth century has repeatedly discovered the actual cities and places mentioned in both of them. Look up the details (see the Bibliography for some important books in this subject).

10. *The piety of Homer and of his characters.*

Suggestions: Note the way Homer talks about the gods, and how his characters think of them (with fear, as Odysseus of Poseidon; with humor, as the Phaeacians of Hephaistos, Aphrodite, and Ares; with awe and religious seriousness, as Odysseus of Athena). Try to construct a full statement about the quality of the Greek religious sense.

SELECTED BIBLIOGRAPHY

Translations

The first English translation of the *Odyssey* is that of George Chapman (1616), whose fine translation of the *Iliad* inspired Keats' famous sonnet ("Much have I travelled in the realms of gold"). There is a fairly readable translation by Thomas Hobbes (1673), the philosopher. Alexander Pope's translation of 1725 is a magnificent poem in its own right. ("It is a pretty poem, Mr. Pope, but you must not call it Homer," said the great Classicist Richard Bentley.) William Cullen Bryant did a translation in 1871.

The first translation made in a modern style was that of Samuel Butler, whose translation is in prose. In effect, he made a hugely readable novel of the *Odyssey*. Other prose translations of the modern period are those of W. H. D. Rouse (who had the critical assistance of Ezra Pound), of E. V. Rieu (Penguin

Books), and of "T. E. Shaw," alias T. E. Lawrence (also Chapman and Ross), the heroic soldier known as Lawrence of Arabia.

There are three important translations of the *Odyssey* into verse in our time: that of Ennis Rees (Modern Library), of Robert Fitzgerald (Doubleday and Co.), and of Richmond Lattimore, in preparation while this handbook was being made (though portions have appeared in magazines; e.g. *Arion*, Winter, 1965). The latter two are highly recommended. Mr. Rees' translation is competent and easy to read, but lacks the tone of the original.

There are many more translations, over the years: some forty by a rough count. Each age makes its own translations.

Useful Studies

Bérard, Victor. *Dans le sillage d'Ulysse*. Paris, 1933. A book of photographs of the world of Homer. Highly recommended for information about the landscape and geography.

_____. *Did Homer Live?* London, 1931. A lively essay on "the Homeric question" as seen by a French scholar. Most interesting for its tentative identifications of the places in Homer's geography and its theory about the origins of the *Odyssey* in the world of the Phoenicians. (This is a translation and adaptation of the author's *L'Odyssée d'Homère*, Paris, 1931.)

de Coulanges, Numa Denis Fustel. *The Ancient City*. New York, 1956 (original edition, 1864). This classic study of the organization of ancient Mediterranean societies, especially the city-state, remains the definitive description of the Greek world. To read this book is to understand what it must have felt like to live in a world of the intricate, pervasive Greek religion and a set of laws that Homer took to be the nature of the universe.

Finley, M. I. *The World of Odysseus*. New York, 1959. This clearly written paperback is a discussion of the manners, morals, laws, customs, in short, the culture that Homer describes. It is both historical and interpretative.

Germain, Gabriel. *Homer*. New York, 1960. A charming, richly illustrated paperback essay on Homer and Homeric times. Translated from the French. One of the best introductions to the subject ever written. Highly recommended for the student just beginning the study of Homer.

Kirk, G. S. *The Songs of Homer*. Cambridge, 1962. Archaeological, literary, and linguistic materials are brought to an analysis of the Greek epic tradition, its genesis and development.

Wace, A. J. B., and F. H. Stubbings, editors. *A Companion to Homer*. New York, 1963. This large and expensive book is the most up-to-date gathering of Homeric information (archeological, linguistic, critical). It is a scholar's book, but it is clear, readable, and concise.

Whitman, Cedric. *Homer and the Heroic Tradition*. Cambridge, 1958. A full discussion of many Homeric themes, by a major scholar. Prof. Whitman is mainly interested in the *Iliad*, but there is much worth knowing here about the *Odyssey*. Recommended for students interested in the form of the epic.

Woodhouse, W. J. *The Composition of Homer's Odyssey*. Oxford, 1930. A scholarly study of how the discrete parts of the *Odyssey* must have been put together. For the student interested in the architecture of the poem's shape.

Other Standard Works on Homer

Allen, T. W. *Homer, Origins and Transmissions*. 1924.

Bassett, S. E. *The Poetry of Homer*. 1938.

Scott, J. A. *The Unity of Homer*. 1921.

Related Studies

Alsop, Joseph, *From the Silent Earth: A Report on the Greek Bronze Age.* New York, 1964. A recent, readable, profusely illustrated account of the excavations at Troy, Pylos, Knossos, and Mycenae, together with the latest interpretations of the finds. The book includes a long interview with the archeologist Carl Blegen.

Carpenter, Rhys. *Folk Tale, Fiction and Saga in the Homeric Epics.* Berkeley, California, 1958. A controversial and fascinating work.

Chadwick, John. *The Decipherment of Linear B.* New York, 1958. The story of Michael Ventris' heroic decoding of the tablets found at Knossos (and later at Pylos and Mycenae) by Sir Arthur Evans at the turn of the century. Chadwick was Ventris' collaborator. A book about the discovery that has caused all ancient history to be seen in a new light.

Hadas, Moses. *A History of Greek Literature.* New York, 1950. First few chapters deal with the oral tradition, Homer, and the epic cycles.

Harrison, Jane. *Prolegomena to the Study of Greek Religion.* Cambridge, 1903. A pioneer study of Greek rites, by a disciple of Sir James Frazer (whose *The Golden Bough*, now out of date, was the first anthropological study of pagan religions). Miss Harrison can tell the student much about the nature of the gods and the meaning of the Greek festivals and rites. Much of the work is outdated.

Kerenyi, Carl. *The Gods of the Greeks.* London, 1951. A more systematic study than the following, describing the organization of religious systems rather than a philosophical interpretation.

_____. *The Religion of the Greeks and Romans.* New York, 1962. A lucid study of what the religions meant, how they worked in their societies. An important book in that it carefully establishes the kind of piety the ancients felt toward their gods and the world.

Lord, Albert B. *The Singer of Tales.* New York, 1965. An account of research by Lord and Milman Parry on the techniques of oral composition of epic poetry.

Onians, R. B. *The Origins of European Thought.* Cambridge, 1951. An advanced book, but astounding in its penetration of ancient physiology and psychology. Homer's concept of the body, of the mind, of time, of fate, of the gods and so forth. The student curious about the distance between his own and Homer's concept of the nature of things is urged strongly to look into this extraordinary study.

Otto, Walter F. *The Homeric Gods,* trans. Moses Hadas. New York, 1954. Discussion of religion in the *Iliad* and *Odyssey.*

Palmer, Leonard R. *Mycenaeans and Minoans.* New York, 1963. The new light thrown on Bronze Age history by the decipherment of the Linear B tablets. Reads like a detective story.

Rose, H. J. *Gods and Heroes of the Greeks.* London, 1957. Useful in understanding the wealth of material with which Homer and the later Greeks had at their disposal out of the extensive mythologies of their tradition.

Vermeule, Emily. *Greece in the Bronze Age.* Chicago, 1964. A scholarly but clear book which makes many aspects of the Mycenaean Age in Greece very vivid.

Zimmern, Alfred. *The Greek Commonwealth.* New York, 1911. The classic study of the economic and everyday life of the Greeks, and of their forms of government.

GLOSSARY

Names and Places in the Odyssey

Achaeans—a general name for all Greeks in Homer, even though the term specifically designates the people of the Peloponnesus.

Acheron—one of the five rivers of the Kingdom of Hades which the dead must cross to enter the underworld.

Achilles—hero of the *Iliad* and greatest of the Greek warriors in the Trojan War; Odysseus meets Achilles' ghost in the underworld (Book XI).

Agamemnon—King of Mycenae and leader of the Greeks at Troy. He is slain on his return to Mycenae after the war by his wife Klaitemnestra and her lover Aigisthos; the murder is the theme of Aeschylus' fifth-century tragedy, the *Agamemnon*. Orestes, son of Agamemnon, later avenges his father's death with the murder of his mother and Aigisthos.

Aiaia—the isle of Circe's palace, at the head of the Adriatic Sea (see MAP, p. 5); *Aiaia* translates from the Greek as "Land of Grief" and here Odysseus and his enchanted men remained for better than a year.

Aigisthos—the lover of *Agamemnon's* wife (see above); comparisons are made between Aigisthos and the suitors of Penelope (as he had enjoyed Agamemnon's wife while that warrior was away at the Battle of Troy, just as Odysseus is delayed in his homecoming; see *Orestes*, below).

Aiolos—god of the winds on whose island (see MAP, p. 5) Odysseus and his men spend a comfortable month as narrated in Book X.

Aias (Ajax)—the Greek warrior at Troy, second in greatness only to Achilles.

Aithiopis—a Greek epic in the Trojan or "Homeric" Cycle dealing with a continuation of the *Iliad* story. It contains the account of the death of Achilles (see COMPLETE BACKGROUND, "Other Greek Epics").

Aktoris—a handmaiden to Penelope.

Alkinoös—King of the Phaeacians and father of Nausikaä. It is at the feast given him by Alkinoös, in Book VIII that Odysseus relates the adventures which comprise Books IX through XII. When Alkinoös learned Odysseus' identity he wished to have him as son-in-law; he nevertheless gave his guest many gifts and safe passage home to Ithaka.

Amphinomos—the suitor whom Odysseus seems to try to warn away in Book XVIII.

Amphithea—Odysseus' maternal grandmother, wife of Autolykos.

Amphitrite—sea nymph and wife of Poseidon; Homer equates her with the sea itself, as in the personification "the dark waves of Amphitrite."

Antikleia—mother of Odysseus; see CHARACTER ANALYSIS.

Antinoös—the chief suitor; see CHARACTER ANALYSIS.

Antiphates—a chief of the Laistrygonians who, in Book X, destroys all of Odysseus' ships but one.

Antiphos—a greek warrior at Troy who sailed homeward with Odysseus but was devoured by Polephymos in Book IX.

Aphrodite—goddess of love and beauty, legend had her born in the sea from the sperm of Uranos' severed testicles when Kronos emasculated his father. In the *Iliad* she had engineered the love of Paris and Helen (the cause of the Trojan War). Aphrodite is the wife of *Hephaistos* and, as might be expected from Homer's occasionally farcical handling of the gods, the goddess of love has love problems herself. She was beloved of Poseidon and herself loved Ares, the god of war. One of the most humorous passages in the *Odyssey* relates (Book VII) of her and Ares being caught, in the throes of love, in Hephaistos' golden net.

Apollo (*or Apollon*)—the god of light, healing, and (in later myth) music; in the *Iliad* he took the side of the Trojans and was instrumental in the death of Achilles. He is a son of Zeus and the brother of Artemis.

Arkeisios—Odysseus' paternal grandfather, thought in some myths to be a son of Zeus by mortal woman.

Ares—the god of war (later the Roman *Mars*), son of Zeus and Hera; he is the lover of *Aphrodite* (above) in the anecdote of Book VII.

Arete—Queen of the Phaeacians, wife of Alkinoös, and mother of Nausikaä.

Arethusa—a nymph and companion of the chaste Artemis, she is pursued in one myth by the river god Alpheos for her beauty; Artemis metamorphoses her into a fountain or spring.

Argives—a term used by Homer, like *Achaeans* and *Danaäns,* to refer to all Greeks, though the term specifically designates the people of Argos.

Argos—(a) Odysseus' faithful dog, Argos dies in Book XVII upon recognizing his master; (b) a region and city north-east of Mycenae in the Peloponnesus (see MAP, p. 10).

Arcadia—a beautiful, mountainous region, haunt of the god Pan, in the Peloponnesus, west of Mycenae (see MAP, p. 10).

Argonautica—Greek epic dealing with the voyage of Jason and the Argonauts (in their ship the *Argo*) in search of the Golden Fleece (see COMPLETE BACKGROUND, "Other Greek Epics").

Artemis—the chaste goddess of the hunt and animals and of pregnancy and the moon; she is the twin sister of Apollo. Homer tells us that Penelope and Nausikaä (and even Helen) greatly resemble her.

Athena—see *Pallas Athena.*

Atlas—the father of Kalypso, he is a Titan (and a brother of Prometheus) who is condemned by Zeus to, at the ends of the earth, hold up the heavens. In later myth Atlas is confronted by Perseus (the Roman *Mercury*) who shows him the head of Medusa; the hideous head had power to turn the beholder into stone and Atlas' name was thus given to the mountain range in North Africa.

Atreus—the father of Agamemnon and Menelaos.

Attica—region in central Greece, whose chief city is Athens (see MAP, p. 10).

Autolykos—Odysseus' maternal grandfather.

Boreas—the north wind.

Calypso—see *Kalypso*

Cassandra—see *Kassandra.*

Charybdis—see *Kharybdis.*

Chios—a rocky island in the Aegean, held by legend to have been a residence of Homer (see MAP, p. 10).

Circe—a daughter of Helios (the sun). She is the witch-goddess of the island of Aiaia who enchants Odysseus' men and transforms them into swine. Odysseus remains with Circe for a year; when he is to leave she directs him to the underworld and warns him of the Sirenes and the cattle of Helios Hyperion.

Cocytus—a river in the underworld.

Ctimene—see *Ktimene*.

Crete—isle south of Greece in the Mediterranean (see MAP, p. 5) held in times much earlier than Homer to have been the Kingdom of Minos (see COMPLETE BACKGROUND, "Geography in Homer"). Excavations there have revealed details of architecture and ornamentation which have led some to consider Crete the isle of King Alkinoös, though Bérard has chosen the modern Corfu as home of the Phaeacians.

Cyclops—a race of one-eyed giants (their name translates from the Greek as "the round eyes"); it is the cyclops Polyphemos whom Odysseus and his men blind and mock in Book IX, thus incurring the wrath of Polyphemos' father Poseidon.

Cypria—Greek epic in the Trojan or "Homeric" Cycle, dealing with Paris and Helen and their flight from Sparta to Troy before the outbreak of the war (see COMPLETE BACKGROUND, "Other Greek Epics").

Danaäns—a general name for the Greeks in Homer.

Delos—isle in the Aegean (see MAP, p. 10), smallest of the Cyclades; sacred to Apollo.

Delphi—place of the oracle of Apollo (see MAP, p. 10).

Demeter—goddess of grain and the mother of *Persephone*; sister to Zeus and Poseidon, she is often called the "Earth-mother."

Demodokos—blind poet at the court of Alkinoös in Book VIII; his name translates from the Greek as "Esteemed by the People."

Diokles—host, at Pherae, of Telemakhos and Pesistratos in Book III.

Dolios—the faithful servant of Penelope who was the father of Melantheus and who, in Odysseus' absence, is an attendant of Laërtes (some scholars consider *Dolios* to be three distinct characters).

Eidothea—sea nymph and daughter of the shape-shifting Proteus.

Elpenor—the youngest of Odysseus' men, it was he who broke his neck on leaving Circe's palace in Book X and his is the first ghost Odysseus meets in the underworld in Book XI.

Eos—the dawn, wife of Tithonos. She has rosy fingers and toes as Homer never tires of the personifying formula "the rosy-fingered dawn."

Erinys—the furies, avenging goddesses with the forms of horrible, sharp-taloned birds.

Euboea—large island off the eastern coast of Attica (see MAP, p. 10), the largest Greek island in the Aegean.

Eurylaos—the Phaeacian youth who taunts Odysseus in Book VII into entering the games.

Eurykleia—Odysseus' and Telemakhos' nurse—see CHARACTER ANALYSIS.

Eurymedousa—Nausikaä's nurse.

Eurynome—a housekeeper in Odysseus' palace.

Eurynomos—a suitor.

Eurylokhos—Odysseus' man who escapes Circe in Book X to tell his leader what has befallen the others.

Eurymakhos—a prominent suitor who, in the plot to murder Telemakhos, makes the deceitful speech to Penelope in Book XVI.

Eurytos—legendary archer and first owner of Odysseus' bow.

Father of Gods and Men—an epithet of Zeus.

Ge (or Gaia)—Mother Earth.

Hades (or Aides or Aidoneus)—brother of Zeus and ruler of the world of the dead.

Halitherses—the Ithakan prophet of Book II who declares that the suitors will soon meet judgment.

Harpies—winged monster-women who snatch away the souls of the dead; not to be confused with the *Erinys* and the *Sirenes*.

Hebe—the goddess of youth and of spring; a daughter of Zeus and wife of Herakles.

Helen—wife of Menelaos and lover of Paris, see CHARACTER ANALYSIS.

Helios Hyperion—the sun; it is his isle in Book XII where Odysseus' men eat of the enchanted cattle against the advice of Circe.

Hellas—a general name for Greece.

Hephaistos—god of fire, a son of Zeus, he is the armor-smith to the gods and the husband of the goddess of love, Aphrodite.

Hera—sister and shrewish wife of Zeus, the goddess of marriage and the family.

Herakles—son of Zeus (his name means "glory of Hera"), he is the legendary performer of the twelve labors. He built, in some myths, the famous Pillars of Herakles and is later the Roman *Hercules*.

Hermes—god of thieves, travel, and commerce; in the *Odyssey* he is messenger to the gods. Hermes is considered the guide of souls into the Kingdom of Hades (he is also the bringer of dreams)—son of Zeus and Maia, goddess of death.

Hyperion—see *Helios*, above.

Ilias Parva—a lost Greek epic of the Trojan or "Homeric" Cycle said to deal with the last days of the Trojan War. It contains the account of the wooden horse of Odysseus (see COMPLETE BACKGROUND, "Other Greek Epics").

Ilium (*or Ilios*)—see *Troy*.

Ionia—Greek Asia Minor in Homer's time.

Ios—the island (see MAP, p. 10) where the oracle at Delphi had prophesied that Homer would die.

Iros—the beggar with whom the disguised Odysseus fights in Book XVIII.

Ismaros—city of the Kikones sacked by Odysseus after leaving Troy (see MAP, p. 5).

Ithaka—home and Kingdom of Odysseus.

Kalliope—the muse of epic poetry on whom Homer calls in Book I.

Kalypso—sea goddess of the isle Ogygia, where she kept Odysseus for seven years. She is a daughter of Atlas and had offered Odysseus immortality which he refused.

Kassandra—daughter of Priam, prophetess and prize of war of Agamemnon. Apollo had offered her the gift of prophesy in return for her favors; when she denied him his pleasure he cursed her that her prophesies would not be believed until too late.

Kharybdis—a monster, known in Greek myth to be the daughter of Poseidon and Ge; she is the alternating whirlpool and waterspout (opposite the six-headed *Skylla*) who sucks in the sea so that the stones of the ocean floor are visible, then spews a geyser forth (Book XII).

Kimmerians, the Land of—entrance to the underworld as narrated in Book XI.

Kronos—son of Uranos and father of the Olympian gods. Kronos was dethroned by Zeus, Hades and Poseidon who then divided his universe among themselves—Zeus taking the sky, Hades the underworld, and Poseidon the sea.

Ktesippos—a wealthy suitor who insults the disguised Odysseus in the feast of Book XX.

Ktimene—Odysseus' older sister (only mentioned, she has no role in the epic).

Lacedaimon—(a) the region of Greece of which Sparta was the chief city, (b) another name for Sparta.

Laërtes—the father of Odysseus, see CHARACTER ANALYSIS.

Laistrygonians—the savages of Book X ruled by King Lamos who destroys all of Odysseus' ships but his own which had been the only one to remain outside the harbor.

Lamos—King of the Laistrygonians.

Lamphos—see *Phaëton*.

Laodamas—son of King Alkinoös and brother of Nausikaä.

Leiodes—the first suitor to attempt to string the great bow in Book XXI.

Lemnos—isle in the Aegean (see MAP, p. 10) said to be the favorite of Hephaistos.

Leukothea—the sea nymph who saves Odysseus' life in Book V by giving him her garment as a buoy in the sea between Ogygia and Phaeacia.

Linear B—the script found on tablets at Knossos on Crete, Pylos and Myceanae in the Peloponnesus and elsewhere (see COMPLETE BACKGROUND), discovered in translation to contain Greek vocabulary but in a non-Greek alphabet.

Lotos—the food of those whom Odysseus and his men meet in Book IX; it was evidently a narcotic and the word translates from the Greek as "forgetfulness."

Maia—goddess of death and mother of Hermes.

Maron—maker of the wine stolen from the Kikones; *Maron, son of Evanthes* translates as "Sage Leaf, son of Pretty Flower."

Medon—a servant in Odysseus' palace.

Melantheus—the unfaithful goatherd; see CHARACTER ANALYSIS.

Melantho—sister of Melantheus, she is a sluttish and disloyal maid.

Menelaos—husband of Helen, King of Sparta; see CHARACTER ANALYSIS.

Mentes—the man whose identity Athena assumes as disguise when she visits Telemakhos in Book I.

Mentor—the disguising identity taken by Athena when she sails with Telemakhos to Pylos.

Minos—legendary King of Crete at Knossos; in Homer, Minos is a judge of the dead in the underworld.

Mycenae—the city ruled by Agamemnon.

Nausikaä—daughter of Alkinoös, she discovers the naked Odysseus washed ashore in Book VI; see CHARACTER ANALYSIS.

Nekuia—a traditional division of the *Odyssey* (see *Telemachiad* and *Nostos*). The *Nekuia* deals with the wanderings and adventures and the descent into Hades, thus encompasses Books V through XII.

Neleus—the father of Nestor.

Nestor—King of Pylos; see CHARACTER ANALYSIS.

Nostoi—a Greek epic in the Trojan or "Homeric" Cycle dealing with the homeward voyages of the Greek heroes (Odysseus has his own *Nostos*, see below).

Nostos—see *Nekuia;* the *Nostos* is that division of the *Odyssey* (Books XIII-XXIV) dealing with Odysseus' return to Ithaka following the narration of his adventures at the court of King Alkinoös.

Notos—the south wind.

Odysseus—see CHARACTER ANALYSIS.

Oedipos—ancient King of Thebes who, as prophesied at the oracle of Delphi, slew his father and wed his mother, bringing a curse upon his city. Oedipos is chief figure of the Theban Cycle of epics.

Ogygia—the isle of the enchantress Kalypso.

Olympos—mountain in Thessaly (a region in Northern Greece) held by the Greeks to be the home of their gods.

Orestes—(see *Agamemnon*, above) murderer of his mother Klaitemnestra and her lover to avenge his father's insult and murder. Homer has Telemakhos learn the story of Agamemnon's death and vengeance that his duty in ridding his mother of the insolent suitors might be emphasized.

Pallas Athena—goddess of wisdom and the intelligence, she is the special guardian of Odysseus and Telemakhos and Penelope. Athena is the daughter of Zeus and is his favorite child. In a sense, Athena is the Olympian counterpart of Odysseus: she the cleverest of the gods, he the cleverest of men. She is described as clear-eyed, bright-eyed.

Patroklos—hero of the *Iliad;* beloved companion of Achilles.

Peisistratos—(a) son of Nestor and companion to Telemakhos, see CHARACTER ANALYSIS; (b) ruler of Athens who, about 540 B.C., appointed a committee of men of letters to edit and establish a standard text of the *Iliad* and *Odyssey* (see COMPLETE BACKGROUND, "History of the Text"); this Peisistratos is said to be a descendant of Neleus and was thus named after Nestor's son.

Peleus—the father of Achilles.

Penelope—see CHARACTER ANALYSIS.

Persephone—Queen of the Dead, wife of Hades and daughter of Demeter. In Greek mythology she is carried off by Hades causing the great sorrow of Demeter (goddess of plant fertility) and a resultant winter on earth. Persephone regularly returns from the underworld to visit her mother, thus the cycle of the seasons.

Phaeacians—a seafaring people ruled by King Alkinoös; when Odysseus is washed up upon their island he is treated royally: entertained and given gifts and safe passage in their ships to Ithaka. By their aid to Odysseus they incur the wrath of the Earth-Shaker, Poseidon.

Phaistos—city of ancient Crete, see COMPLETE BACKGROUND, "Geography in Homer."

Phaëton and Lamphos—horses, according to Homer, which drew Helios' sun-chariot.

Phemios—the minstrel accompanying the suitors.

Philoitios—Odysseus' cowherd; like the faithful *Eumaios,* he stands with Odysseus in the slaying of the suitors in Book XXII.

Polites—Odysseus' most loyal sailor.

Polybios—(a) a father of the suitor Eurymakhos, (b) a suitor himself; these do not seem to have been the same man.

Polyphemos—leader of the one-eyed giants and sons of Poseidon. A prophet had once warned him that "Odysseus" would come to put out his eye; the prophesy is realized in Book IX. The Greeks sailed safely away from the land of the Cyclops but the wrath of Polyphemos' father was to follow them thereafter.

Poseidon (*or Poseidonos*)—god of the sea, brother of Zeus and Hades, he is the father of the cyclops Polyphemos and is known by the epithet "Earth-Shaker." Later to become the Roman *Neptune*, he lives in the underwater palace near Euboea and his wrath against Odysseus becomes the mainspring of the epic's plot.

Priam—King of Troy.

Proteus—a sea divinity and a god of Metamorphosis (a "shape-shifter").

Pylos—chief city of Nestor's kingdom, visited in the *Odyssey* by Telemakhos; it is possible that this is the same city excavated in modern times, revealing samples of the Linear B script discussed in the COMPLETE BACKGROUND (see MAP, p. 5).

Rhexenor—father of Arete, he is the brother (and father-in-law!) of Alkinoös.

Sicily—see *Thrinakia*.

Sirenes—sea nymphs, half-women and half-birds, they sing so enchantingly as to lure sailors to their island, lure ships onto their rocky coast to their destruction. Odysseus and his men, the latter with their ears sealed and Odysseus lashed at his request to the mast, pass them safely in the first adventure narrated in Book XII.

Sisyphos—said in some myths to have ravished Odysseus' mother and thus been his father; Odysseus meets him in Hades in Book XI where Sisyphos' punishment is to roll a massive stone up a hill; eternally he does this and eternally the stone slips away from him and rolls back down.

Skylla—the six-headed monster, opposite the monster *Kharybdis*, in Book XII. Odysseus was faced with the choice of losing his entire ship to Kharybdis or six men to Skylla—six of his best men were snatched away, screaming and wriggling like fish in the jaws of the monster. In some legends Skylla was said to have once been a beautiful maiden, changed by Circe in a jealous rage over the love of one of the gods of the sea.

Sparta—also called *Lacedaimon*, chief city of the Kingdom of Menelaos, husband of Helen.

Styx—one of Hades' five rivers, so sacred that the gods often make their oaths by it.

Tantalos—another of the tortured souls seen in Hades (Book XI) whose punishment is to stand, eternally thirsty, in a pool or river; whenever he stoops to drink the water recedes and from this we have taken the word "tantalize."

Tartaros—the deepest, darkest part of the Kingdom of Hades; it is here that Sisyphos labors.

Teiresias—blind seer of Thebes who prophesied the doom of King Oedipos, above. In Book X Circe advises Odysseus that he must descend to the underworld and consult the spirit of Teiresias to learn of that which lay before him. In Book XI, Teiresias warns Odysseus not to kill the cattle of Helios Hyperion and tells him of the state of affairs in Ithaka.

Telemakhiad—(see *Nekuia* and *Nostos*), a traditional division of the *Odyssey*, encompassing Books I through IV, and Book XV, dealing with the journey and adventures of Telemakhos.

Telepylos—the city of King *Lamos*, above.

Thebes—ancient city of King Oedipos (see MAP, p. 10).

Theoklymenos—the prophet of Pylos who, fleeing from his home in Argos, sails with Telemakhos in Book XV.

Thetis—sea nymph, mother of Achilles.

Thrace—district at the northern end of the Aegean (see MAP, p. 5) of which Ismaros, city of the Kikones, is a coastal settlement sacked by Odysseus as narrated in Book IX.

Thrasymedes—a son of Nestor.

Tiryns—coastal city of Argos, mentioned in the *Iliad*, excavated in modern times (see COMPLETE BACKGROUND, "Geography in Homer" and MAP, p. 10).

Thrinakia—(see MAP, p. 5) an ancient name for Sicily as the Greek translation implies "three corners"; considered to be the land of Helios Hyperion visited by Odysseus and his men in Book XII.

Troy—city of Priam and Paris in the Troad, a district in Asia Minor; also known as *Ilios* or *Ilium*.

Zephryos—the west wind.

Zeus—father of gods and men, chief of the Olympian gods; a sky-god, he is known by many epithets: "high-throned," "lord of lightning" (his weapon is the thunderbolt), "aegis-bearing," "dark-clouded." In the *Iliad* and the *Odyssey* Homer gives Zeus the dimensions of a good man who has an extraordinarily tempestuous family (and a tragic and complex world of men) to look after and lead toward righteousness and balance as best he can. Zeus later becomes the Roman *Jupiter*.

NOTES

NOTES

NOTES

NOTES

NOTES